CONSTITUT

ADMINIST

Q&

Private Law Tutor Publishing
Foreword

Thank you for buying this book. The problem that I encountered when studying law is: knowing everything. There is so much to read and so little time to do it. If you skip some material, or a case you are none the wiser. So throughout my years teaching law I have devised a system and I am going to share this with you.

You may have encountered different methods or formulas to help when advising a client in a mock scenario. One of example is the *IRAC* method or another is *Celo*. These are well documented and you can read about these. I never used them, because I had a method in my head that worked. It was not until I started teaching that I spoke about it. I call my method the "**Fact Law Sandwich**". Let me explain. If you are asked to advise a party as to their legal rights this is how you present it:

FACTS
GENERAL PRINCIPLE
LAW
APPLY TO FACTS

In **Fact:** simply state what you have been told, this why you can never be accused of not considering the facts. In **General principle:** you simply state what the general rule of the relevant issue is. You express it as if you are speaking to a child who has no knowledge of law. In **Law**: you state "using the authority of…..and you go on to state which statute or case helps prove your point. Lastly in **Apply to Facts**: you apply the reasoning of the case to your factual scenario. Your advice will sound and look structured and professional. The reason it is called the "Fact Law Sandwich", is because the advice contains two outer layers of facts that sandwich the principle and law in the middle.

This book is written to provide the student with a good knowledge of the most important cases on their study. It is written in a way to facilitate the Fact Law Sandwich method. I provide the general principle, the name of the case with full citation, the facts, the Ratio (the thing the lecturers say you always need to use), and application i.e. how the case should be applied. No other book provides this information at your fingertips. I hope you enjoy using it.

CONSTITUTIONAL & ADMINISTRATIVE Q&As

Private Law Tutor Publishing

Chapter 1 - Welcome/Introduction/Overview

This book provides you with basic information as a basis for you to form your own critical opinions on this area of law. Once you have mastered the basics, you will be inspired to question principles in your essays and apply them in mock client advisory scenarios. Again, for your convenience, we have provided you with examples of how to answer such questions and how to apply your knowledge as effectively as possible to help you get the best possible marks. This aid is a fully-fledged source of basic information, which tries to give the student comprehensive understanding of how to answer questions for this module.

The aim of this Book is to:

- Provide an introduction to anyone studying or interested in studying Law to the key principles and concepts that exist in this module.
- To provide a framework to consider the law in this module within the context of examinations or written work.
- Provide a detailed learning resource in order for legal written examination skills to be developed.
- Facilitate the development of written and critical thinking skills.
- Promote the practice of problem solving skills.
- To establish a platform for students to gain a solid understanding of the basic principles and concepts of in this module, this can then be expanded upon through confident independent learning.

Through this Book, students will be able to demonstrate the ability to:

- Demonstrate an awareness of the core principles;
- Critically assess challenging mock factual scenarios and be able to pick out legal issues in the various areas of this module;
- Apply their knowledge when writing a formal assessment;

- Present a reasoned argument and make a judgment on competing viewpoints;
- Make use of technical legalistic vocabulary in the appropriate manner; and
- Be responsible for their learning process and work in an adaptable and flexible way.

Studying this module

This question and answer series covers core subjects that the Law Society and the Bar Council deem essential in a qualifying law degree. Therefore, it is vital that a student successfully pass these subjects to become a lawyer. The primary method by which your understanding of the law will develop is by understanding how to solve problem questions. You will also be given essay questions in your examinations. The methods by which these types of question should be approached are somewhat different.

Tackling Problems and Essay Questions

There are various ways of approaching problem questions and essay questions. We have provided students with an in-depth analysis with suggested questions and answers.

Chapter 2 - The Characteristics of a Constitution

Essay Question 1

The constitution is a necessary requirement in every state. It is the document that the Government draws its power and gives legitimacy to its actions. Discuss

Answer

Introduction

This question calls for an assessment of the unique situation in countries without a written constitution. The following discussion will focus on the widely debated unwritten constitution of the UK. The advantages and disadvantages of such a constitution will be evaluated and arguments will be made to determine whether or not there is a need for a written constitution in the UK.

According to **Professor K C Wheare** a constitution is "the whole system of government of a country, the collection f rules which establish and regulate or govern the government." **Thomas Paine's** view on the constitution reveals more complex ideas as according to him "...a government without a constitution is a power without right...A constitution is a thing antecedent to a government; and a government is only the creature of a constitution." A constitution therefore establishes the rules providing for the powers, functions and limits of the three organs of the government (that is, the legislative, executive, and judiciary), the fundamental rights of citizens as well as the relationship between the government and citizens. In many countries these rules are stated in a single document. In the UK however, the constitution is derived from many written and unwritten sources that are both legal and non-legal. It is therefore more accurate to term the British constitution uncodified.

In order to understand why UK does not have a codified constitution, it is necessary to understand UK's historical, legal, and political landscape, that despite having gradually evolved over centuries, has not actually experienced a sudden drastic change or break. For example, Malaysia has a codified constitution because it was given independence by the British in 1957 to become an independent state and The United States of America went through a revolution during the 18th century. Although there have been significant cataclysmic events in the British history such as the 17th century English civil war, these happened almost a century before the idea of a written constitution began to seriously take form in the late 18th century. By then, UK was well past the major changes and Parliament sovereignty was established so any new changes that occurred were easily dealt with acts of Parliament.

One of the main advantages an uncodified constitution offers is flexibility. With an uncodified constitution, it is easy for the legislators to make and unmake laws of constitutional importance. In the UK there is no special procedure to repeal or amend statutes of constitutional importance other than getting a simple majority in Parliament. For example, in the UK, the landmark case of **Somersett** aided by a well-organized abolitionist movement ended the practice of owning slaves in England and contributed to Parliament enacting the Slavery Abolition Act in 1833. In the words of **Hillaire Barnett**, "In the UK, constitutional changes can be brought about with the minimum of constitutional fuss." In contrast, countries with a written constitution have to jump through several hoops before amendments to the constitution can be made. For example in Malaysia, amendments to the Federal Constitution require a 2/3 majority in the 'Dewan Rakyat' (House of Commons). In addition, if the matter has to do with the national religion of Islam and the special position of Malays there is a further requirement where approval from the Council of Malay Rulers must be sought. This point can be viewed differently in that the whole idea of a codified constitution in the case of UK may be against the model of democratic representation. Democracy dictates that the contending parties put out their wares for the public's perusal and eventual choice during elections. If the majority agrees to a particular party's election manifesto and the party forms the new executive then in the name of democracy, it must be allowed to carry out its election promises with minimal fuss. However, with a codified constitution, only a constitutional amendment may allow certain policies to be implemented and this is just a tedious process as mentioned above.

Another merit of an uncodified constitution is the sovereignty of Parliament. The UK Parliament is the sole legislative body and cannot be bound by its predecessors nor can it bind its successors. However, in countries with a written constitution, there is usually a constitutional court that will decide on the validity of government policies and legislation. This will inevitably lead to the judiciary being dragged into matters pertaining politics. A clear example of this is the case of **Roe v Wade** which is a landmark decision legalising abortion. The United States Supreme Court held that abortion was protected under the 14th Amendment. Other than the obvious issue of abortion, this decision also fuelled debates regarding the lines (or lack thereof) between constitutional adjudication and legislating. Another instance would be the **Dred Scott** decision in the United States Supreme Court. The court here held that slaves were too inferior to have any rights that the "white man" had to respect. Ultimately this resulted in the Missouri Compromise, which banned slavery in the Northern territories of the 36°30' parallel, being overturned. The crux of the matter is simply that judges are not elected by the people the way ministers are and cannot be said to truly represent the people. Therefore, there is no reason that they should act in the capacity of legislators. However, in the current times of constitutional upheaval in UK in regards to the independence of Scotland (referendum in 2014) it is suggested by John Drummond that the point should be shifting sovereignty to the people and not Parliament.

The current chairman of the Constitutional Commission pressure group, John Drummond heavily credits the Thatcher government for truly exposing the constitution as a convenient arrangement for the exercise of power.

As mentioned briefly earlier, the arbitrary protection of citizen rights is another flaw in having an uncodified constitution. This is because the rights of the citizens are not entrenched in a Constitution. Instead it exists in the form of a statutory act (Human Rights Act 1998) that can be very easily repealed by a simple majority n Parliament. According to **A.V. Dicey** the rule of law is the best protector of fundamental rights and a Bill of Rights is unnecessary so long as there are courts. This coupled with Parliament's legislative power constitute UK's fundamental rights. This is illustrated by the case of **Entick v Carrington**. In this particular case, the King's Chef Messenger was ordered by the Secretary of State to search Entick's residence by force. Entick was suspected of writing and publishing seditious material. Entick sued for trespass. The court held that the Secretary of State had no right under statutory or common law to issue a warrant for search and found in favour of Entick. It is argued that while A. V. Dicey is right to a certain extent, his point on courts upholding citizens' rights does not always hold true. For example, in the case of **Malone v MPC**, the police tapped Malone's phones on the authority of a warrant issued by the Home Secretary. Malone sued the police for a violation to his right of privacy. The court held that there was no such right under English law (this was prior to the HRA 1998). More recently this year after the Snowden revelations showed that British intelligence GCHQ has secretly gained access to the network of cables which carry the world's phone calls and internet traffic and has started to process vast streams of sensitive personal information which it is sharing with its American partner, the National Security Agency (NSA). Although still under investigation, the allegations if true, reveal the extent to which rights in the UK are arbitrarily protected, or as John Drummonds puts it, depending on the government of the day. It can be counter-argued however, that the existence of an entrenched document does not guarantee a protection of human rights and to think so is to be overly optimistic. Countries such as Somalia have a written constitution but cannot be said to uphold the rights of its citizens by any means. A written constitution is only as valuable as the government of the day deems it to be. Without political will it is merely a litany of words with little meaning.

When weighing the pros and cons listed above in relevance to the UK particularly, it must be highlighted that the issue is rather complex and is not limited to two polar options of codifying or not codifying. According to Rodney Brazier, there are four options to be considered when evaluating the need for codification. The most conservative course of action will naturally be to allow the gradual evolution of the constitution by building on existing laws and conventions as it is currently and historically. This method is reactive and is applied as and when needed. At the other extreme is to put in place a complete codification of rules that will result in a proper codified constitution in a single document. However, a less considered option situated between the extremes exist. One option is to consolidate the Labour Governments efforts in constitutional reform of the UK's uncodified constitution has been developed over time to become one of the most successful governing systems in the world as evidenced by its political stability and efficient executive, legislative and judiciary systems in place. It is dynamic due to the flexibility accorded by an uncodified constitution and this has enabled it to grow and change bit by bit. It has its fair share of faults but then again, so does every system. The UK has a system that works well despite these flaws and its long history is proof enough that this is a system that rectifies itself before it becomes too inefficient or unjust. Furthermore, codification of the UK constitution is a task of unimaginable magnitude and will consume a lot of time and money that I dare say, is rather unnecessary in the current situation. The only matter with any sense of urgency is regarding the rights of UK citizens, as any country that is truly democratic will ensure its citizens' rights are always protected. However, in my opinion having an entrenched Bill of Rights, without codifying the entire constitution, is a satisfactory solution. I disagree however, with the notion that what isn't broken should not be fixed. The point being that it is far from prudent to what for a cracked glass to shatter before anything done. However, in developing the constitution, a slow evolution is better than radical changes.

Essay Question 2

Should the United Kingdom now codify its constitution? Critically discuss.

Answer

Codifying the constitution

This essay will discuss the opportunity to codify the UK constitution pointing to the variety of options available. First, it define the UK constitution and discuss what is the meaning of writing or codifying the constitution. Second it will discuss the merits and demerits of modifying the constitutional arrangement as it pertains to the Legislative, focussing on Parliamentary Sovereignty the introduction of strike down clauses, the Parliamentary validation of Prerogative powers and the balance of power between Parliament and the courts. Third, it will discuss the merits and demerits of reforming the constitution as it pertains to the Executive, separation of power between the Executive and Parliament and the codification of conventions and the protection of rights.

The UK uncodified constitution

According to the cabinet manual, 'a constitution is about public power, the power of the state. It establishes the institution of government states their principal powers and regulates the exercise of those powers in a broad way'. The House of Lords Constitution Committee adds that a constitution is 'a set of laws and practices that stipulate the relationship between the different institutions and the individual'. The UK constitution has some key features. It is derived from many written (The Bill of Rights, the Act of settlement, the Parliament ACT 1911 and 1949...) and unwritten (Conventions, Prerogative Powers ...) sources whish are legal and non-legal. The UK does not have a higher law, so Parliament decides what is constitutional. There is no required process of constitutional amendments, such as referendums or special majority voting.

Codifying the constitution

Depending on the definition of codifying or writing the UK constitution, engaging in such an exercise may in fact produce a variety of outcome. There are a variety of constitutional reform options which would all have different impact on the constitutional arrangement in the UK each with its own merits and demerits. To illustrate this point, The Political and Constitutional Reform Committee of the House of Commons presented recently a research document 'A New Magna Carta?' lays out options for constitutional reform, which are as follows:

(1) Constitutional Code - a document sanctioned by Parliament but with no statutory authority, setting out the essential existing elements and principles of the constitution and workings of government. Such a document would have little impact on the current constitutional arrangement but arguably could have the benefit of improving the clarity of the constitution.

(2) Constitutional Consolidation Act - a consolidation of existing laws of a constitutional nature in statute, the common law and parliamentary practice, together with a codification of essential constitutional conventions. The greatest impact of such document would be to render legally binding and enforceable by the courts conventions, which in turn would give more power to the courts vis a vis the Executive.

(3) Written Constitution - a document of basic law by which the United Kingdom is governed, including the relationship between the state and its citizens, an amendment procedure, and elements of reform. Depending on the substance of this document it could have the greatest impact on all Branches of Government and in particular modify significantly Parliamentary Sovereignty.

Codification and Parliamentary Sovereignty

Arguably the UK most important constitutional principle is the doctrine of Parliamentary supremacy (PS). The debates pertaining to codifying the UK constitution and PS revolve around the issues of creating entrenched 'higher laws' and granting the courts strike-down power. Oliver argues that PS and the entrenchment of 'higher laws' are mutually exclusive and that such a development would effectively amount to 'parliamentary suicide'. Indeed according to the orthodox definition of Dicey P can make and unmake any laws it wishes and cannot bind its successors.

In turn, the courts, staffed by unelected judges, would be charged with assessing the compatibility of new laws produced by elected members of P against the constitution. This would amount to a significant transfer of power to the courts. Lord Neuberger argues that such a move would be undemocratic and lack political accountability.

An accompanying concern it that a move towards a politization of the judiciary could unfold with Judges acting as legislators, as was arguably the case in the US where in the case *Wade v Roe* the courts decided that abortion was protected under the 14th Amendment and thereby blocked an elected US congress from enacting legislation aiming at curbing abortion.

Another concern developed by Blick is that the process of codification could undermine the flexibility of the current constitutional arrangement which does not provide for special amendment procedures and thus allows the constitution to adapt to changing political and social circumstances. In contrast, amending the US constitution required a 2/3 majority vote and approval of 2/3 of the US States. Although a majority of American voters seek a curb on gun laws the protection of the right to bear Arms under the 2nd amendment has posed a challenge to reform in this area.

There are four counter arguments to this view

First, Hokman argues that PS and constitutional codification are not necessarily incompatible. Indeed, it is possible to have entrenched laws to implement a system that falls short of giving the courts power to strike down laws. For example, the courts could be given the power issue a declaration of incompatibility, or Parliament requested to implement an express repeal procedure. Parliament would retain its power to amend or not the specified law.

Second, the current constitutional arrangement has arguably already moved away from the orthodox arrangement described by Dicey. Jack Straw acknowledged that indeed entrenching 'higher laws' would run against the orthodox definition of PS but that Dicey's orthodox definition of the UK constitution does not accurately describe the current constitutional arrangement. Indeed, the rule of law has emerged as a competing basis of the constitutional arrangement as evidenced by Devolution, the CRA 2005, the HRA or the process of European integration. Although Parliament remains legally supreme in theory its practical power to legislate and to have courts give full effect to P intention has been restrained. For example, the HRA grants courts power to interpret laws consistently with the ECHR, as far as possible, and issue a DOI if they find a law incompatible. Moreover in *Jackson*, the courts have established that EU law is supreme over UK laws. In obiter, Judges argued that PS was a common law construct and that the ultimate source of PS was the trust the people placed in Parliament, pointing to an existing tension between the Judiciary and the Legislative power.

Third, the process of judicial review although falling short of granting courts power to challenge P decisions has allowed them to challenge the process by which laws and decisions, practically granting the courts quasi legislative power. In *Bland*, the courts ruled on whether unplugging a life support machine was murder and in *R v R* whether marital rape was illegal. In *Shaw v DPP* the courts ruled that they had common law power to enforce the purpose of morality of laws.

Fourth, Eleftheriadis controversially argues that the UK constitution may in fact be both a flexible and extremely rigid constitution, by the mere fact that it is impossible to make a change from an uncodified constitution to a codified one. Also, a counter argument to the rigidity of special amending procedures has not prevented other constitutions from evolving over time.

Codification of Power and the Executive

The debates on the codification of the constitution and the Executive revolve around the notions of Separation of power and the protection of individual rights.

Lord Hailsham has described the UK parliamentary system as one of an "elective dictatorship". According to the theory of executive dominance, the executive effectively controls parliament both due to the first-past-the-post system which gives it a disproportionately large majority ensuring that government bills are rarely rejected and the use of party whips to pressure potentially dissident MP's into supporting their party. Despite the bicameral nature of parliament devolution of power away from the House of Lords means that there are few checks on the House of Commons. When taken together with the executives effective dominance of the commons this means that the executive effectively dominates the legislature in the UK.

In addition the executive also have use of the Crown's prerogative powers, which parliament has little control over or conventions such as the Salisbury convention which lack clarity and certainty.

The codification of constitutional conventions would arguable minimize the dangers of uncertainty and abuse by giving them greater legitimacy and authority. Further codification would afford greater clarity which would facilitate access to the constitution for members of the public who are arguably entitled to understand the law that governs them.

It may be argued that without further codified constitution the executive's powers remain unfettered. Codification of the constitution would effectively limit the executive's powers as well as afford additional protection to key acts such as the ECA 1972 and HRA 1998 which theoretically could be unilaterally repealed through executive pressure in parliament.

Chapter 3 – The Nature and Sources of the UK Constitution

Essay Question 1

With regards to Sources of the British Constitution, please describe those most peculiar to the UK in their non-legal nature, and the extent to which they are used.

Answer

Introduction: Background

A constitution can straightforwardly be defined as, the body of rules and arrangements that regulates the government of a country. Lawyers in the United States of America can access their constitution in a single document in which the rules of governance lie catalogued. To further understand his constitution he must look to law reports where the Supreme Court has given substance to the meaning of rules through it decisions. **Marshall & Moddie** say finally to grasp a more informed understanding, a lawyer will also have to examine non-legal rules which are set on the constitution to fill in the gaps.[1] The use of a written constitution in any civilised society is to ensure a balance of rights, awareness, and authority. A constitutional lawyer in the United Kingdom faces a more cumbersome task of hunting for our unwritten constitution in a number of places and forms. **Rodney Brazier** say he will have to look in legislation, case law, European community law, non-legal rules, statements about the royal prerogative, practises of parliament, and internal rules of political parties.[2] For the British constitutional lawyer matters are less clear-cut and uncertainty exists as to precisely which one of these forms has constitutional importance. The only realistic approach he could take is to consult literature on the constitution by authoritative writers, this however is a subordinate source, and it can be appropriate to use as a last resort.

---

[1] G. Marshall & G.C. Moddie, *Some Problems of the Constitution*, 5th edn., 1971, London: Hutchinson, p. 13-14

[2] Rodney Brazier, *Constitutional Reform*, 2nd edn., 1998, Oxford: OUP, p. 2.

Non-legal rules: constitutional conventions

A major difficulty surrounds constitutional lawyers in reference to non-legal rules of constitutions. The non-legal rules termed conventions, are defined by **AV Dicey** as '...*understandings, habits, or practices which,...regulate the conduct of the several members of the sovereign power, of the Ministry, or of other officials...* '[3] Conventions in reality are not seen as laws, the lack of legal substance detach conventions from law courts, hence, they are of no concern to courts and lawyers. **AV Dicey** put it 'As a lawyer I find these matters to high for me.'[4]. Although conventions are not enforceable in courts, they have demanded recognition. In a case concerning the publication of dead minister's memoirs, in a newspaper, the breach of convention was distinguished as a line of persuasion, but could not be seen be the court as a binding authority.[5] **Marshall & Moddie** say once having recognized the role of conventions, a lawyer of the British Constitution, further faces the job locating the documentation of these rules, those can be found in the preamble to the relevant Act, reports of the imperial conferences or the conferences of the Prime Minister, where these rules, are officially decided and documented.[6]

What amounts to a constitutional convention?

As way of a starting point, conventions according to **AV Dicey** are defined as: "*...conventions, understandings, habits or practices which, though they may regulate the conduct of the several members of the sovereign power...are not really laws at all since they are not enforced by the courts. This portion of constitutional law may, for the sake of distinction, be termed the 'conventions of the constitution', or constitutional morality...*" This definition concentrates on what conventions are supposed to achieve. However, this view is not entirely accurate and it is important that

---

[3] Dicey, A.V., *Introduction to the Study of the Law of the Constitution,* 10th edn., 1959, London: Macmillan, p. 24

[4] *Ibid.* p.21

[5] *Attorney-General v. Jonathan Cape Ltd* [1976] QB 752

[6] Marshall, G. & Moodie, G.C., S*ome Problems of the Constitution,* 5th edn., 1971, London: Hutchinson, p. 25

17

conventions are distinguished from mere habits and practices. Conventions are conceptually different from habits or practices in that these concepts do not prescribe or dictate what ought to happen but are merely descriptive of what in fact does happen. A Further definition of the purpose of conventions was given by **Sir Ivor Jennings** as: "*The short explanation of the constitutional conventions is that they provide the flesh that clothes the dry bones of the law; they make the legal constitution work; they keep it in touch with the growth of ideas.*" To that end, it is a characteristic of constitutions in general that they contain some areas which are governed by conventions, rather than by strict law. However a simplistic characterization of constitutional conventions, moreover, for discussion purposes regarding this quandary, **Fenwick's,** definition seems to be most appropriate, Fenwick stated: "*Conventions may be roughly defined as non-legal, generally agreed rules about how government should be conducted and, in particular, governing the relations between different organs of government*".

Example of Constitutional convention: Collective ministerial responsibility

A constitutional convention exists in the doctrine of collective ministerial responsibility. **Tomkins, A** describes this convention as: "*The convention of collective responsibility means that all ministers in the government must accept responsibility for the policies, decisions, and actions of the government, even if they did not personally develop or take them, and even if they personally disagree with them.*" This convention forces an obligation on all ministers of the government to support and defend government policy. It is expected that ministers 'speak in one voice' and to adopt a position of collective responsibility. The purpose of this convention is to give an impression of government unity, moreover, to give the public confidence in their policies. Ministers are not expected to be outspokenly critical of government policy. Ministers who find a particular policy unacceptable should resign from office.[7]

---

[7] An example of this occurred over the Iraq War in 2003. Foreign Secretary Robin Cook resigned after failing to accept collective responsibility for the decision to commit Britain to military action in Iraq

Duty of confidentiality

Another facet of collective responsibility is namely, that all ministers owe their cabinet colleagues a duty of confidentiality. It is a conventional obligation for ministers to keep what's debated or argued within the cabinet, *'in house'*. To break this confidentiality obligation would seriously undermine the unanimity rule and also inhibit Ministers from speaking their minds. This rule is generally seems to be abided, however press reports of cabinet discussions are published with sufficient regularity, suggesting that in practice in tends to be overlooked by some ministers. A more controversial issue is whether this confidentiality obligation should be maintained following a minister's departure from the cabinet. Furthermore, if so, for how long and how stringently should this obligation be adhered to? This predicament came before a court of law in *Attorney General v Johnathan Cape Ltd and Others*[8] popularly known as the *Crossman Diaries* case.

Attorney-General v Jonathan Cape Ltd and Others

The question before the court in this case was; whether or not the courts would enforce the convention of cabinet secrecy? In this case, Crossman who was a member of the cabinet between 1964 and 1970 kept a detailed account of cabinet government in operation, in the form of a comprehensive diary. His intention was to publish his accounts, subsequent to his retirement. However, sadly Crossman died prematurely; however, his wife decided to continue in his legacy and publish the diaries. After publications appeared in the tabloids, the government sought an injunction preventing further publications. The Government argued that the courts should seek to preserve the confidentiality of governmental affairs. Crossman's publishers argued that the doctrine of cabinet confidentiality was merely a moral obligation, which ministers could regard or disregard according to their own ethics. To that

---

without international agreement or domestic support. Mr Cook could not back the governmental stance regarding the war with Iraq. Furthermore, he publicly criticised the government's involvement in the campaign. With this in mind, conventional rules demanded his resignation.

[8] [1976] QB 752

end, in this case, **Lord Widgery CJ**, did not find history a beneficial guide, as per **Lord Widgery**: *"I find overwhelming evidence that the doctrine of joint responsibility is generally understood and practiced, and equally strong evidence that it is on occasion ignored".*

Lord Widgery went on to deliver a somewhat perplexing judgement. Firstly he accepted that ministers owed each other a legally enforceable duty of confidentiality. However this duty did not derive from the convention turning into law. It was created by 'stretching' the existing common law parameters. However, in this case it was held that due to the lapse in time, the material had lost its confidential quality. Technically, this case was not an example of a court enforcing a convention, but accepting that a convention was coincidentally underpinned by existing common law rules. In functionalist terms, it could be argued that the courts enforced a convention by cloaking it with a common law label. In addition this case is not the only example of conventions being taken into account by the courts. In **Liversidge v Anderson and Carltona Ltd v Commissioner of Works**,[9] the courts supported the refusal to review the grounds on which executive discretionary powers had been exercised on the basis that a minister is responsible to parliament for the exercise of his power. In light of this, the relationship between law and convention is brought to the forefront. Furthermore, it is now possible to consider whether conventions can crystallise into laws, or indeed whether this would be of any benefit.

Can conventions be legally binding?

In theory all conventional rules of the constitution could be enacted in legal form by parliament. Moreover, there have been times when constitutional conventions have been given legal status. An example of a conventional rule attaining legal status occurred following a breach of convention by the House of Lords between 1908 and 1910. One major conventional rule regulated the relationship between the House of Lords and the House of Commons in legislative matters and most particularly in financial matters: namely that the Lords would ultimately give way to the

---

[9] [1943] 2 All ER 560

will of the commons. This convention broke down in 1908, when the House of Lords rejected the finance bill of the Commons. After a deadlock, the government responded to this and introduced the Parliament Act 1911. The act set the prior convention in legal stone and provided that the House of Lords would no longer enjoy equal powers to approve or reject legislative proposals and that its power would be restricted to a power to delay legislation subject to strict time limits. To that end, it can hereby be seen that where a breach of a convention is deemed sufficiently severe, parliament can, in the exercise of its sovereign supremacy, change a convention into a legal rule.

Conclusion

Having now established that constitutional conventions can be placed on a statutory basis, several questions start to arise. If conventions are binding why not codify them? Or conversely, if conventions are obeyed why bother to codify them? The answer to both questions respectively ultimately lies in ascertaining whether or not there would be any great advantage in codifying constitutional conventions.

Essay Question 2

Is it time to abandon the principle of a constitutional convention and rather change constitutional conventions into legally binding rules? Critically discuss.

Answer

Introduction

Firstly this paper will look at the different definitions of what amounts to a constitutional convention, and to their function or purpose. Second this paper will consider different examples of constitutional conventions. Third this paper will discuss whether or not it would be possible or even useful, to change constitutional conventions into legally binding rules.

What amounts to a constitutional convention?

As way of a starting point, conventions according to AV Dicey are defined as:

"conventions, understandings, habits or practices which, though they may regulate the conduct of the several members of the sovereign power...are not really laws at all since they are not enforced by the courts. This portion of constitutional law may, for the sake of distinction, be termed the 'conventions of the constitution', or constitutional morality..."

This definition concentrates on what conventions are supposed to achieve. However, this view is not entirely accurate and it is important that conventions are distinguished from mere habits and practices. Conventions are conceptually different from habits or practices in that these concepts do not prescribe or dictate what ought to happen but are merely descriptive of what in fact does happen. A Further definition of the purpose of conventions was given by Sir Ivor Jennings as:

"The short explanation of the constitutional conventions is that they provide the flesh that clothes the dry bones of the law; they

make the legal constitution work; they keep it in touch with the growth of ideas."

To that end, it is a characteristic of constitutions in general that they contain some areas which are governed by conventions, rather than by strict law. However a simplistic characterization of constitutional conventions, moreover, for discussion purposes regarding this quandary, Fenwick's, H, definition seems to be most appropriate, Fenwick stated:

"Conventions may be roughly defined as non-legal, generally agreed rules about how government should be conducted and, in particular, governing the relations between different organs of government"

Retrospectively therefore, it appears that the U.K constitution as a whole is comprised of two categories. The first category consisting of the legal rules of the constitution, as found in case law, statute and subordinate legislation, which preside over society as a whole. The second, consisting of Political and moralistic non-legal rules or constitutional conventions that are accepted as binding within society, despite not enforceable in a court of law. Though these conventions are not set in Legal stone, their existence over the years has invariably lead to smooth operation of government.

Examples of Constitutional Conventions

The Royal assent

It is a convention that the queen will accept the legislation passed by the government. In theory the queen could refuse to give the royal assent to a bill proposed by the government. However, it is almost beyond belief that she would refuse to do so for the constitutional crisis this would create would be catastrophic. The public revolt against an unelected person rejecting legislation that a democratically elected government has put forward would be seen as constitutional suicide. In light of this, it is just accepted in the modern era that the queen will give all parliamentary legislation the royal assent.

Peter Mandelson

In addition, it is a convention that a Minister of the crown should be a member of parliament. In general, if a the prime minister wishes to appoint someone to ministerial office who is not yet an MP, he/she will either have to be offered a peerage to the House of lords, or given an early opportunity to win a seat in the House of Commons via a by-election, However there are a few established exceptions to this conventional rule.

Collective ministerial responsibility

Another constitutional convention exists in the doctrine of collective ministerial responsibility. Tomkins, A, describes this convention as:

"The convention of collective responsibility means that all ministers in the government must accept responsibility for the policies, decisions, and actions of the government, even if they did not personally develop or take them, and even if they personally disagree with them."

This convention forces an obligation on all ministers of the government to support and defend government policy. It is expected that ministers 'speak in one voice' and to adopt a position of collective responsibility. The purpose of this convention is to give an impression of government unity, moreover, to give the public confidence in their policies. Ministers are not expected to be outspokenly critical of government policy. Ministers who find a particular policy unacceptable should resign from office. A recent example of this occurred over the Iraq War in 2003. Foreign Secretary Robin Cook resigned after failing to accept collective responsibility for the decision to commit Britain to military action in Iraq without international agreement or domestic support. Mr Cook could not back the governmental stance regarding the war with Iraq. Furthermore, he publicly criticised the government's involvement in the campaign. With this in mind, conventional rules demanded his resignation.

Duty of confidentiality

Another facet of collective responsibility, is namely, that all ministers owe their cabinet colleagues a duty of confidentiality. It is a conventional obligation for ministers to keep what's debated or argued within the cabinet, '*in house*'. To break this confidentiality obligation would seriously undermine the unanimity rule and also inhibit Ministers from speaking their minds. This rule is generally seems to be abided, however press reports of cabinet discussions are published with sufficient regularity, suggesting that in practice in tends to be overlooked by some ministers.

A more controversial issue is whether this confidentiality obligation should be maintained following a minister's departure from the cabinet. Furthermore, if so, for how long and how stringently should this obligation be adhered to? This predicament came before a court of law in *Attorney General v Johnathan Cape Ltd* popularly known as the *Crossman Diaries* case.

Attorney General v Johnathan Cape Ltd

The question before the court in this case was; whether or not the courts would enforce the convention of cabinet secrecy? In this case, Crossman who was a member of the cabinet between 1964 and 1970 kept a detailed account of cabinet government in operation, in the form of a comprehensive diary. His intention was to publish his accounts, subsequent to his retirement. However, sadly Crossman died prematurely; however, his wife decided to continue in his legacy and publish the diaries. After publications appeared in the tabloids, the government sought an injunction preventing further publications. The government argued that the courts should seek to preserve the confidentiality of governmental affairs. Crossman's publishers argued that the doctrine of cabinet confidentiality was merely a moral obligation, which ministers could regard or disregard according to their own ethics. To that end, in this case, Lord Widgery CJ, did not find history a beneficial guide, as per Lord Widgery:

"I find overwhelming evidence that the doctrine of joint responsibility is generally understood and practiced and equally strong evidence that it is on occasion ignored"

Lord Widgery went on to deliver a somewhat perplexing judgement. Firstly he accepted that ministers owed each other a legally enforceable duty of confidentiality. However this duty did not derive from the convention turning into law. It was created by 'stretching' the existing common law parameters. However, in this case it was held that due to the lapse in time, the material had lost its confidential quality. Technically, this case was not an example of a court enforcing a convention, but accepting that a convention was coincidentally underpinned by existing common law rules. In functionalist terms, it could be argued that the courts enforced a convention by cloaking it with a common law label. In addition this case is not the only example of conventions being taken into account by the courts. In *Liversidge v Anderson and Carltona Ltd v Commissioner of Works*, the courts supported the refusal to review the grounds on which executive discretionary powers had been exercised on the basis that a minister is responsible to parliament for the exercise of his power. In light of this, the relationship between law and convention is brought to the forefront. Furthermore, it is now possible to consider whether conventions can crystallise into laws, or indeed whether this would be of any benefit.

Can conventions be legally binding?

Constitution of Canada

The question of whether a convention could materialize into a law was raised in the case of *reference re amendment of the Constitution of Canada*. Native Indians claimed that the *Canada Act 1982* was *ultra vires*, on the grounds that their consent had not been sought. It was argued by the native provinces the convention of obtaining provincial consent prior to the passing of legislation, had crystallised into a law. Therefore the legislation passed without the consent of the provinces was invalid. By majority, the Canadian Supreme court recognised the constitutional convention. Nonetheless, the court went on to hold that no convention could limit the legislative capacity of parliament. The Supreme Court held that the consent of the provinces was not required by law, and again by majority, that the consent was required by convention, but the convention could not be enforced by a court of law.

Example of conventions made legally binding?

However, in theory all conventional rules of the constitution could be enacted in Legal form by parliament. Moreover, there have been times when constitutional conventions have been given legal status. An example of a conventional rule attaining legal status occurred following a breach of convention by the House of Lords between 1908 and 1910. One major conventional rule regulated the relationship between the House of Lords and the House of Commons in legislative matters and most particularly in financial matters: namely that the Lords would ultimately give way to the will of the commons. This convention broke down in 1908, when the House of Lords rejected the finance bill of the Commons. After a deadlock, the government responded to this and introduced the Parliament Act 1911. The act set the prior convention in legal stone and provided that the House of Lords would no longer enjoy equal powers to approve or reject legislative proposals and that its power would be restricted to a power to delay legislation subject to strict time limits. To that end, it can hereby be seen that where a breach of a convention is deemed sufficiently severe, Parliament can, in the exercise of its sovereign supremacy, change a convention into a legal rule.

Having now established that constitutional conventions can be placed on a statutory basis, several questions start to arise. If conventions are binding why not codify them? Or conversely, if conventions are obeyed why bother to codify them? The answer to both questions respectively ultimately lies in ascertaining whether or not there would be any great advantage in codifying constitutional conventions.

In Australia, a constitutional crisis in 1975 contributed to an experiment in codification of conventions into an authoritive but non-legally binding text. During the crisis, conventions had been 'creatively interpreted and ignored' in an attempt to unseat the labour government in the depths of an international recession. In 1983, a plenary session of the Constitutional convention adopted a set of 34 'practices' which were to be 'recognised and declared' as conventions of the Australian constitution. However, Professor Charles Sampford analysed the merits and demerits of this codification and he found there to be many problems and unanswered questions. Furthermore it was seen, codification is, even if desirable, by no means straight forward.

Chapter 4 - The Separation of Powers

Essay Question 1

Is there a fair balance between judicial responsibilities in the way the courts interpret law to produce the right outcome and the separation of powers in that the legislature is the only body allowed to make law.

Answer

This paper will determine if there is a fair balance between judicial responsibilities in the way the courts interpret law to produce the right outcome and the separation of powers in that the legislature is the only body allowed to make law. It will first argue the point that legislation is most appropriate because the court can overlook or misapply the law. Second it will argue using case law we should have a formalist rule of law. It will look at case to show that the rule of law and separation of powers collectively control discretion and arbitrary power. Lastly the paper will show how human right are protected through both the judiciary and legislature.

Barendt argues if all three branches of government (judicial, legislative and executive) rest in one body without checks and balances this can be can be tyrannical. The courts can overlook a law or discriminatingly apply laws against certain groups or individuals.[10] One example is **Mandla v Dowell-Lee**.[11] In this case a school had refused to admit a Sikh student because he had a turban. The school denied that being a Sikh was a membership of a racial or ethnic group. Lord Denning dissented and held this case should not have been perused. The decision classed Sikhs as not being "ethnic". Lord Denning remarks sparked protests, including a demonstration where thousands of Sikhs participated in Hyde Park. Ministers were forced to intervene and declare that if the House of Lords did not correct the Court of Appeal ruling they would legislate to remedy the problem. Craig thus argues the judgements of the courts are starting to resemble those of

---

[10] Barendt, "Separation of Powers and Constitutional Government"
[1995] *Public Law* 599
[11] [1983] UKHL 7

politicians and administrators and violated the separation of powers.[12]

Unger argued that the formalist rule of law was a way of legitimising rules of law that preserved inequality in society.[13] The formal rules of law cannot be sustained in post-liberal society where the state needs to intervene in more and more areas of life and therefore laws have to be left unclear so as to permit the government to intervene in as many ways possible, and therefore the judiciary are left to interpret laws through purposive reasoning, taking into account the intended aims of the legislation, the perfect evidence of which is the **Pepper (Inspector of Taxes) v Hart**[14] ruling.

If judges proceed as they think fit they are participating in a legislative function, which violates the separation of powers.[15] Lord Reid stated: *"To apply the words literally is to defeat the obvious intent of the legislature. To achieve the intent and produce a reasonable result we must do some violence to the words".*[16] However, Kavanagh argues legal certainty requires that we apply the law as it is written form and do not look for some "wider meaning".[17] One example was the interpretation of the Restriction of Offensive Weapons Act 1959 in **Fisher v. Bell**.[18] The decision was so unwelcomed by Parliament that they overruled it by statute the same year. In **Burmah Oil v Lord Advocate**[19] the judiciary held the UK government was accountable for damages for destroying oil fields during war. Parliament responded by legislating the War Damages Act 1965 to avoid the liability bestowed on them by the judiciary. In **Anisminic Ltd. v. Foreign**

---

[12] Craig, "Formal and Substantive Conceptions of the Rule of Law: An Analytical Framework" [1997] PL 467
[13] Craig, "Formal and Substantive Conceptions of the Rule of Law: An Analytical Framework" [1997] PL 467
[14] [1992] UKHL 3
[15] Verkuil, Paul R., "Separation of Powers, the Rule of Law and the Idea of Independence" [1988] *Wm. & Mary L. Rev.* Vol 30, 301.
[16] **Luke v. Inland Revenue Commissioners** [1963] A.C. 557 at p. 577
[17] Kavanagh "Pepper v Hart and Matters of Constitutional Principle" [2005] 121 LQR 98
[18] [1961] 1 QB 394
[19] [1965] AC 75

Compensation Commission,[20] a statute prevented *"decisions"* of the Commission from being *"called in question in any court"*. Despite parliament's intention the court held the decision was ultra vires, and void. This demonstrates the courts are free to proceed as they think fit and check the lawfulness of decisions. We can conclude that parliamentary sovereignty is dependent on the judiciary's acquiescence of Parliamentary power.

Raz says that through the rule of law, laws should be prospective, open, certain and capable of guiding human conduct.[21] However these formal rules do not guarantee that laws suiting the needs of the people will actually be met and should be balanced against society's other needs. Others prefer a more substantive doctrine including conformity to human rights. Under s.3 Human Rights Act 1998 the courts obligation is to interpret all domestic legislation with Convention rights *'so far as it is possible to do so'*.[22] This is a teleological method of interpretation, where the spirit of the Treaties is given effect to.[23] If the court feels unable to interpret in this way a declaration of incompatibility under section 4 of the 1998 Act is made. This provision reasserts parliament has the final say.

Essay Question 2

Prerogative powers represent one of the most fundamentally significant areas of constitution law, not least because of their definitional difficulties. However, the most controversial aspect remains controlling their use. Discuss.

Answer

Prerogative powers have developed into a significant source of the UK constitution. Like most of the other type of elements that make the constitution, it is not enlisted as a formal text in any single

---

[20] [1969] 2 AC 147
[21] Raz, Joseph, "The Politics of the Rule of Law" (1990) Ratio Juris 3, No: 3, 331-339.
[22] s.3 Human Rights Act 1998
[23] Brown, L.N. and Kennedy, T. *The Court of Justice of the European Communities*, 4Ed., London: Sweet & Maxwell, 1994

document and may appear less constructive. However, when it comes to the definition of Prerogative powers, Dicey's offering in this matter is not hard to grasp – *'... the residue of discretionary or arbitrary authority, which at any time is legally left in the hands of the Crown ... Every act which the executive government can lawfully do without the authority of an Act of Parliament is done in virtue of this prerogative[24].'* With regards to Blackstones[25] and Joseph Chitty's[26] definition of the prerogative and Dicey's version provides us the following –

- Prerogative powers are inherent and exclusive to the Crown
- It is a production of Common Law and these powers are residual ie pertaining from other law
- These powers are commonly and widely used by the Executive for the Crown
- Exercise of Prerogative powers do not require authority from an Act of Parliament

Examples of Prerogative powers include the appointment and dismissal of Prime Minister and other Ministers, the appointment of Queen's Counsel and senior judiciary, granting honours, citizenship and passports etc – (Domestic); the making of treaties the declaration of war, the deployment of the armed forces on operations overseas, the recognition of foreign states, the accreditation and reception of diplomats, restrain aliens entering the UK – (Foreign affairs).

Outlining prerogative powers becomes much easier with recent Parliamentary Publications mentioned below. However, the more important task of controlling the use of such power is both a political and legal undertaking. In the following part of this essay,

---

[24] [1885, p 424] – Constitutional & Administrative Law, Fifth Edition, Hilaire Barnett, Cavendish Publishing, chp6, p 124

[25] *Commentaries* (1765-69) by Blackstone define Prerogative powers as – *'that special pre-eminence whicht the King hath over and above all other persons....'*

[26] Joseph Chitty [1820, p2] defines Prerogative power as *'the rights of sovereignty........distinct from the people at large'*

Political and Judicial control of Prerogative powers are focused upon.

Since the Bill of Rights 1688 and Crown Proceedings Act 1947, Parliament can expressly remove a prerogative powers and may wish to enact a substitute statute. However, in the context of Parliamentary Democracy where accountability of government and scrutiny of politicians' every actions are held to be absolutely important; the exercise, application, scope and limitations of Prerogative powers has in the recent years attracted a lot of attention. Referring to the uncodified UK constitution, perhaps not entirely out of nature, a list of Prerogative powers used by the government was published only in 2003 for the first time by the CPAC[27], obtaining information from the Department of Constitutional Affairs. And it was in 2003, leading up to the British invasion of Iraq, the then Labour Government led by Tony Blair placed unprecedented political strain on the prerogative power 'to declare war on a foreign state'. It was established believe that Parliament would only have an 'advisory' role in the exercise of such an important prerogative belonging to the Crown. However, ex-Prime Minister Tony Blair sought parliamentary approval for the British participation in the war against Iraq. Blair indicated that in the absence of an approval from the parliament he would not lead the Commons to formally advise the Queen to exercise her prerogative power in reaching a decision to declare war. Following this, it was firmly confirmed that Ministers acting under prerogative powers would be politically accountable to the Parliament. Within the Parliamentary political sphere it stirred up actions and counter actions with some pursuant to place statutory and legal limitations of Royal Prerogative. Amongst others, Clare Short[28] proposed a Private Members Bill to remove the declaration of war from the list of Royal prerogative powers and proposed to solely empower the parliament for such a task.

---

[27] Commons Public Administration Committee - PASC PUBLISHES GOVERNMENT DEFENCE OF ITS SWEEPING PREROGATIVE POWERS - Move could help bring bigger say for Parliament - Public Administration Select Committee (PASC 19); session 2002-03; press notice 19;

[28] Clare Short, the then Secretary of State for International Development 2003

But it is the Judiciary that intervened on more number of occasions in the Legal sphere, to place limitations on the exercise of prerogative powers. In the historically significant *Case of Proclamation*[29], Courts strongly argued that they possessed the right to determine the limits of the Royal prerogative. In *BBC v Jones*[30]it was held that no new prerogative powers can be created. In *GCHQ*[31], an argument centering an Executive motion[32], that prerogative powers and instructions issued under delegated power emanating from the prerogative, were discretionary; hence non-justiciable and non-reviewable by the Courts; was dismissed establishing that such Executive motion and delegated power emanating from the prerogative is not necessarily immune to review or justification in the Court of law[33]. Also, it was provided that such powers are subject to limitations by the Court of law. As far as limiting the application and scope of prerogative powers exercised by the Executive it must be noted that modification to these powers were nevertheless, permitted in *ex parte Northumbria Police Authority*[34] and may be applied in line with the Queens power to 'keep the peace in her realm' which on this occasion allowed the Home Office to adopt measures such as to equip the Police forces with Plastic batton rounds and CS gas.

The Courts can also impliedly render a prerogative suspended by relying or giving way to a more appropriate statute provision. In *De Keyser's*[35] the Crown's discretionary power to award compensation to those affected by the emergency seizure of

---

[29] *Case of Proclamation* (1610) EWHC KB J22

[30] The British Broadcasting Corporation (BBC) -v- Johns (HM Inspector of Taxes) [1965] Ch 32 CA; [1964] EWCA Civ 2; [1964] 41 TC 471; (1964) 43 ATC 38; [1964] 1 All ER 923; [1964] 2 WLR 1071; [1964] TR 45; [1964] RVR 579; [1964] 10 RRC 239

[31] Council of Civil Service Unions and others v Minister for the Civil Service [1984] 3 All ER 935

[32] An oral instruction by the Prime Minister issued under article 4 of the Civil Service Order in Council 1982

[33] per Lord Fraser and Lord Brightman in Council of Civil Service Unions and others v Minister for the Civil Service [1984]

[34] R v Secretary of State for the Home Department, ex parte Northumbria Police Authority [1989] 1 QB 26 (CA),

[35] *A.-G. v. De Keyser's Royal Hotel* [1920] AC 508

properties in course of the defence of the realm, was suspended by a more generous compensation scheme provided by a relevant statute. In limiting the Executive's exercise of prerogative powers, the Courts have also held ministerial advice given to the Crown, up for review when that advice was based on an error of law in *ex parte Bently*[36].

Prerogative powers have best suited its application at times of grave emergency. These set of powers are designed to properly apply and respond to a vast possible number of situations may be previously unseen and unprecedented. With the above control measures in place it is for the betterment of transparent accountable democracy that scrutiny and controlling mechanisms are in place. And it is perhaps for the greater good that these historical, unique powers are delegated from the Crown and also retained by the Crown exclusively in appropriate arrangement of the modern British Constitution.

---

[36] *R. v. Home Secretary, ex p. Bentley* [1994] QB 349

Chapter 5 - The Rule of Law

Essay Question 1

With reference to relevant case law, evaluate the extent to which the UK judiciary has demonstrated a willingness to uphold the requirements of the rule of law.

Answer

The definition of Rule of Law is highly debated by academics. This essay will explain the main theories of the Rule of Law and it will analyse what avenues are available to the UK courts to uphold it and how they have dealt with past cases. It will also deal with the closely related issue of separation of powers as it is highly relevant to the control of discretion of both the executive and the judiciary.

Theories of the Rule of law

There are several well-known theories on the rule of law; however, one of the most popular is Dicey's theory. His theory is about the equality of the rules that are enforced by the courts on people. It includes some important principles, which were very influential in the nineteenth century. Such as the official's decisions can be challenged in courts and that the law determines how much power they have or it gives them[37]. Dicey set out three important principles: 1) the absolute supremacy of regular law. Here, Dicey says that if an official has no backing of a specific law, he cannot interfere with another's rights as they are merely agents of the state. Dicey believed that government should not have wide discretionary powers; he argued that it is crucial to have limits and controls over exercising it. This can be said to be exercised to some extent by the court's powers of judicial review. He thought that punishment should only be through the courts and no other way. However, this is not the case today as other bodies such as local authorities have the power to punish in ways such as issuing

---

[37] Cavers, David F. "A Critique of the Choice-of-law Problem." *Harvard Law Review* (1933): 173-208.

fines[38]. 2) Equality before the law – every man is subject to the law of the realm. Dicey believed that no one is above the law and no man including and especially government officials should have any immunity from the courts. He did not mean that officials do not have special powers because this would be untrue, he meant that no matter whom it is, from the prime minister down, they are no different from any other citizen and should be held responsible for their actions without any legal justifications. 3) No higher law other than the rights of individuals as determined through the courts[39]. However, the third tenant of his theory can be criticised on the basis that today we have the HRA in the UK and therefore the courts do not create the fundamental rights[40]. In most countries, the courts only apply the constitution and it does not result from it.

There are, however other theories of the rule of law. Raz believes that the rule of law should be seen in formal terms, which means that the law should be prospective, stable, open, general and clear. There should be access to courts, as well as independent judiciary[41]. His theory was for the rule of law to enable people to plan their lives. He was not concerned with the substance of the law, but the form in which it is enacted. This leads to the paradox of a dictatorship being compliant with the Rule of Law as long as the laws are enacted following the correct procedure and present certain characteristics given that the content is irrelevant[42].

Dworkin agrees with the formal conception of the rule of law, however, he had two different conceptions of the rule of law. The 'rule book' conception is based on the idea that government power should be exercised against individuals only if it is in accordance with previously set rules that are available to all [43]. The second conception is the 'rights' conception, where he argues that citizens

---

[38] Jennings, Ivor. *The British Constitution*. CUP Archive, 1967.
[39] Dicey, Albert Venn. *Introduction to the Study of the Law of the Constitution*. Macmillan, 1897
[40] Kavanagh, Aileen. *Constitutional Review under the UK Human Rights Act*. Cambridge University Press, 2009.
[41] Raz, Joseph. "The rule of law and its virtue." (1977).
[42] Hart, *The concept of law*. Oxford University Press, 2012.
[43] Dworkin, Ronald. *Taking rights seriously*. Harvard University Press, 1978.

should have moral rights and duties to one another, and political rights against the state, so the courts through the demand of citizens can enforce them[44]. Due to this conception being concerned with the moral rights of individuals and the public conception of individual rights, it can be said that Dworkin's conception of the rule of law as a whole is concerned with both form and substance.

Lord Bingham in reiterated the same approach in his work "The Rule of Law'. He lists eight factors which are core to the rule of law and it is evident that they combine both procedural and substantive aspects of the law, in line with Dworkin's approach[45]. The factors identified by Lord Bingham are: the law must be as easy as possible to get access to and predict; the exercise of discretion should not resolve any questions of liability, but only by the exercise of law; the law should be applied equally to everyone; ministers and public officials have been given granted a benefit, therefore, they must use it to exercise power in good faith and fairly to everyone without exceeding their limits and reasonably; fundamental human rights must be protected by the law; if parties cannot resolve any dispute the state must find a way to do so; the procedure used by the judges to make decisions must be fair; the state should comply with the ROL not only on a national level but also internationally[46].

Due to the comprehensiveness of Dworkin's and Lord Bingham's theories, it is submitted that the Rule of Law is not only formal but also substantive. The enactment of the ECHR and the HRA 1998 in the United Kingdom clearly proves that the rule of law is also about the substance of fundamental rights, which the courts are required to enforce.[47]

Unwritten constitution v written constitution

---

[44] Dworkin, Ronald. *POLITICAL JUDGES AND THE RULE OF-LAW.* 1979.

[45] Bingham, Lord. "The rule of law." *The Cambridge Law Journal* 66.01 (2007): 67-85.

[46] Bingham, Tom. *The rule of law.* Penguin UK, 2011.

[47] Ewing, Keith D. "The Human Rights Act and Parliamentary Democracy." *The Modern Law Review* 62.1 (1999): 79-99.

In most countries the system of checks and balances is unlikely to change because it is a constitutional document, which is protected by a special procedure. For example, in the United States, the court can avoid a law passed by the congress if they believe it is inconsistent. Furthermore, even if the president nominates the Supreme court judges, they are appointed by the congress[48].

However, this is slightly different in the UK because there is no written constitution. In the case of *Thoburn v Sunderland City Council*[49] it was clear that some Acts have been recognised as having constitutional status, which in this case was the European communities Act 1972. It was held that constitutional statutes could not be reversed unless they were express words to that degree in the statute, unlike ordinary statutes, which could be reversed by later clashing with Parliamentary statutes.

Rule of Law v. Separation of Powers, in particular judicial independence

The rule of law and separation of powers together are a way of controlling arbitrary power and discretion. Firstly, even though there is no absolute doctrine of separation of powers it may be too vague to say that there is no separation of powers in the UK[50]. There are many different statutes that support the idea of separation of powers in the UK, in particular with regard to judicial independence, such as tenure - provided for judicial security of tenure; immunity – judges cannot be sued; open courts – 'justice must be seen to be done'; political independence and judicial appointments. In The Court Act 1981 it is stated that judges could be removed from position by Parliament but this is not so the case with the government. The Act of settlement 1700 further supports the independence of the judiciary. The existence of such Acts since 1700 shows that Judicial independence and

---

[48] Marshall, Thurgood. "Reflections on the bicentennial of the United States Constitution." *Harv. L. Rev.* 101 (1987): 1.

[49] [2002] EWHC 195 (Admin)

[50] Verkuil, Paul R. "Separation of Powers, the Rule of Law and the Idea of Independence." *Wm. & Mary L. Rev.* 30 (1988): 301.

separation of powers have existed for a long time. Another important role is in article 6 of the European Convention on Human Rights which protects the rights to a fair trial[51].

However, some cases such as *Shaw v DPP*[52] seem to suggest that the judiciary makes new law in contrast with the principle of separation of powers. Here the appellant was charging both the prostitutes and the customers a fee for publishing the prostitutes contact details as well as the services they offer and nude pictures. The court held that he was living on the earnings of prostitution and because of that he was convicted of corrupting public morals, as well as an offence under the Obscene Publications Act 1959[53]. He appealed arguing that no offence such of conspiracy to corrupt public morals exists. He was unsuccessful with his appeal as the House of Lords dismissed it and created a new crime. Another example is seen in the case of *R v R* where a man was charged with the attempted rape of his wife. Although the couple were separated for a long time, they were not divorced. The House of Lords overturned the exceptions of rape and changed the law.

In the case of *Burmah Oil v Lord Advocate*[54], the judges decided that the UK government was liable for damages committed during the war. Parliament then passed the War Damages Act 1965 in response to the judgement, to avoid the effect of the new law created by the judiciary. Looking at these given examples it could be concluded that even though the courts sometimes make new laws, parliament is always ultimately liable and therefore this does not defeat separation of powers. The separation of the judiciary from the other branches may therefore not be necessary.

How the courts ensure compliance with the rule of law

Even prior to when the HRA 1998 came into force, the courts

---

[51] Woodhouse, Diana. "United Kingdom The Constitutional Reform Act 2005—defending judicial independence the English way." *International Journal of Constitutional Law* 5.1 (2007): 153-165.

[52] [1962] AC 220

[53] Edwards, S. S. M. "On the contemporary application of the Obscene Publications Act 1959." *Criminal Law Review* (1998): 843-853.

[54] [1965] AC 75

made it clear through the principle of legality, that the statutes would conform to fundamental rights[55]. This means that fundamental rights could not be overridden by general words and parliament would have to state clearly in the legislation if they intend to limit fundamental rights.

In perhaps one of the most popular modern day cases of *M v Home Office*[56], it is clear that everyone including government ministers are required by the ROL to accept and obey the courts orders. Here, M was to be deported, however, this was not to happen until the hearing of the appeal, which the Home Secretary agreed to. M was deported. The Court ordered for M to be taken off the plane and brought back when it stopped in Paris. Despite the Courts order, the Home Secretary did not feel an obligation to do so and thus M was not taken off the plane. It was held that the Home Secretary had disrespected the Court and was held in contempt of it but no punishment was imposed.

The court might read a statute down in accordance to the Human Rights Act 1998 if the particular statute breaks the terms from the European Convention on Human Rights. If the court felt unable to do so according to section 3 of the HRA 1998, they could issue a declaration of incompatibility under section 4 of the HRA, which would then be sent to Parliament to be reconsidered.

In the case of *A V Secretary for the Home Department*[57] 10 men considered to be a threat to national security by Special Immigration Appeals Commission were ordered to leave the country. They appealed (as they have a legal right to) and argued that in section 23 of the antiterrorism, crime and security act (ACSA) 2001 to detain foreign terror suspects was definitely incompatible with the articles of the ECHR. Their Lordships agreed and issued a declaration of incompatibility, under section 4 of the Human Rights Act 1998. Parliament then replaced the ACSA 2001 with the Prevention of Terrorism Act 2005 that allows anyone no matter his or her nationality to be detained.

---

[55] Jowell, Jeffrey, "The rule of law and its underlying values" *The changing constitution* 6 (2007): 5-23.
[56] [1994] 1 AC 377
[57] [2004] UKHL 56

The case above shows that under the doctrine of Parliamentary sovereignty, Parliament always retains the last word on the legality of an Act[58]. New laws can always be passed to make what was legal, illegal, and nobody, including courts has the power to invalidate these Acts of Parliament. However, in the case of *R (on the application of Jackson) v Attorney General*[59] it has been argued that section 3 and 4 of the HRA 1998 may have affected and questioned how absolute Parliamentary sovereignty is.

We could at present maintain that the courts overall have significant interpretive procedures available to them to guarantee that legislation neglecting to meet the requirements of the rule of law set out above are hardly constructed in favour of the individual.

If the provision that fails to comply with the rule of law is something other than a statute, the courts will have nothing preventing them from invalidating other measures, whether they take the form of delegated legislation, individual ministerial decisions, acts of local authorities or decisions of agencies. The courts use judicial review to invalidate any measure that does not comply with the rule of law[60].

Further, in *Council for the Civil Service Unions v Minister for the Civil Service [GCHQ]*[61], the House of Lords held that executive action is not immune from judicial review even when carried out in pursuant of a power derived from the royal prerogative. However, in this specific case the court had no jurisdiction to review the order as national security, the ground on which the prerogative order relied, was considered to be unjusticiable.

---

[58] Forsyth, Christopher. "Of fig leaves and fairy tales: the ultra vires doctrine, the sovereignty of Parliament and judicial review." *The Cambridge Law Journal* 55.01 (1996): 122-140.

[59] [2005] UKHL 56

[60] Salzberger, Eli, and Paul Fenn. "Judicial independence: Some evidence from the English Court of Appeal." *The Journal of Law and Economics* 42.2 (1999): 831-847.

[61] [1983] UKHL 6

Conclusion

This essay has first analysed the definitions given by various academics of the Rule of Law and has argued that Dworkin's and Lord Bingham's formal and substantial approach to it is the most appropriate to explain the doctrine as applied to modern time taking into consideration the ECHR and the HRA 1998. It has further analysed the tools available to the court both prior and after the enactment of the HRA 1998 to uphold the requirements of the Rule of Law. Prior to the HRA 1998, the court used the principle of legality to create a hardly rebuttable presumption against the breach of fundamental rights. In fact, only expressed words in a statute could override fundamental rights, and the reading of the law, as far as possible, was to uphold those rights. After the enactment of the HRA 1998, the English courts were given an additional tool to enforce fundamental rights, namely the power to issue a declaration of incompatibility under s 4 of the HRA 1998. This essay has presented case law illustrating the applicability of various tools. Further, the courts have a power of judicial review to annul executive actions in breach of fundamental rights. The English court has shown a great willingness to use the tools available to it to uphold the requirements of the Rule of Law. However, this essay has also shown that, due to the doctrine of Parliamentary Sovereignty, the English Parliament retains the final say and can override judicial findings of incompatibility by enacting later legislation as it was the case in *A V Secretary for the Home Department*.

Chapter 6 – Parliamentary sovereignty

Essay Question 1

Has Parliamentary Sovereignty Been Eroding? Critically discuss.

Answer

This essay will show how Parliamentary Sovereignty has defined by Dicey has been challenged in recent years. First, it will present Dicey's definition. Second it will show how EU case law and the UK joining the EU established the supremacy of EU law over UK law in areas covered by EU Law and how the UK courts responded to such developments. Third, it will show that how devolution, the HRA, the concept of constitutionalism articulated in the Jackson case also challenge PS. Finally it will present academic arguments evaluating PS as it stands today.

Dicey

A classic definition of PS was provided by A V Dicey in his Study of the Law of the Constitution. This doctrine articulated three critical elements: First, Parliament is the supreme Legislature, consistently with Art 9 of the Bill of Rights, which states that Parliament decisions may not be challenged by any authority whether courts of monarch. Second, Parliament can make and unmake any law. Third, Parliament cannot bind its successors.

The UK Membership of the EU.

The development of EU case law since the 60' established the supremacy of EU law over member State Law. The UK Parliament was aware of this fact when jointing the EU in 1972, which in turn has challenged PS.

Supremacy of EU law over national laws of the Member of the EU was established by a number of judgements of the European Court of Justice. *Van Gend en Loos* establishes that the European Community is a new legal order for whose benefits member states have limited their sovereign rights. The European Court of Justice deemed Dutch Law inconsistent with Article 12 of the European Community Treaty, which is directly effective in Member States. *Costa v Enel* confirms that EC treaties carry with them a clear limitation of sovereign rights. *IHG* specifically addressed the question of the supremacy of EU law over national laws by establishing that national law cannot override EU Law. *Simmenthal* established that EU law had authority in protecting the rights of individual citizens. The consequence being that national laws could be set aside pre-empted and made to comply with EU law.

Parliament enacted the **European Communities Act 1972** prior to formally joining the EC on Jan 1 1973 giving effect to the EU Treaty (and the accompanying body of past and future EU law) in the UK. (As a dualist state the UK must give effect to treaties by enacting law in the UK). The ECA 1972 contains two provisions structuring the relationship between UK and EC law. First, section 2 of the Act it established that EC law would be directly applicable and enforced in the in the UK. Second, Section 2(4) establishes the primacy of EC law over present and future UK Law.

Although UK courts had an early reluctance to acknowledge the supremacy of EU Law contained in the Act, the interpretations evolved overtime. In *MacCarthy v Smith*, Lord Denning gave EU law indirect effect, rather than direct effect, arguing that EC law should be used as a method of statutory interpretation of UK law. The implication of giving EU Law direct effect is that when inconsistent with EU Law, UK law would have to be set aside and if EC law is sufficiently clear, it should be directly applied. This view arguably conflicts with the rulings in Costa and Van Gend which establish the supremacy of EU Law. In *Factortame*, the House of Lords gave direct effect to EU law. In brief, the case involved a conflict between the provisions of the Merchant Shipping Act 1988, which restricted the registration of fishing vessels as British to those with sufficiently British ownership and crew, and the freedom of establishment as protected by the EC Treaty. It was held that since it was a requirement of the EC Treaty that domestic courts should enforce any provision that had direct effect, the inconsistent national law should be set aside. The Lords established that Section 2(4) of the 1972 Act was to be interpreted as EC law prevailing over UK law. Where the MSA was inconsistent with the ECA, the MSA was not to be applied and EU law to be giving effect instead. Clear words of Parliament were not enforced by the courts.

Courts went even further in **Thoburn**, the courts argued that the 1972 Act (as well as other acts such as the HRA) have a special status. Due to their constitutional value and can only be expressly repealed by Parliament. There could be no implied repeal for constitutional or fundamental acts such as the ECA, but also the HRA. This notion runs against Dicey's orthodox doctrine of implied repeal which provides that new laws prevail over old law. Yet, Theoretically Parliament retains the power to repeal such laws, thus maintaining intact its sovereignty.

In addition, EU regulations are directly enforceable in Member states and Directives can also have a direct effect. This means that they have effect in member states without the need further enactment of legislation by member states legislature. Also, the introduction of qualified majority voting at the EU level means that the UK has less power to veto legislation that would be contrary to its interests. So as long as the 1972 act is effective P has surrendered its sovereignty with regards to areas covered by EU law.

PS is affected in that the enactment of the ECA points to Parliament not only acknowledging another source of legal authority that is the EU, thereby no longer being the sole legislature, but also Parliament is binding itself. Arguably, these developments undermine the Dicean notion that Parliament is the sole legislature, can make and unmake any law and cannot binds its successors.

Yet, although membership of the EU and a number of Act of Parliaments have indeed challenged Parliamentary Sovereignty, Parliament still has the power to restore its original supremacy by repealing the 1972 Act or any other Act. In fact the **European Union Act 2011** reaffirmed that sovereignty lay with the British Parliament, with section 18 stating that directly applicable or directly effective EU law referred to in section 2(1) of the European Communities Act 1972 are given effect in the United Kingdom only by virtue of that Act.

The HRA

The HRA 1998 gives effects in the UK to the rights contained in the European Convention on Human Rights. Two of its articles namely Arts 3 and 4 have an effect on PS.

a) The HRA has been carefully crafted to maintain PS, at least formally. Art 3 provides that Acts of Parliament must be interpreted in a way that is compatible with the ECHR 'as far as it is possible'. *Ghaidan* posits that Parliament intended individuals to be able to enjoy the ECHR rights without any further action of Parliament. However, if an Act of P is significantly inconsistent with the ECHR and does not lend itself to interpretation in the sense that this exercise would amount to amending the act as a measure of last resort the courts can issue a Declaration of Incompatibility.

The act provisions falls short of giving the courts the right to strike down an Act deemed incompatible. The DOI is an invitation by the courts to reconsider an Act, but Parliament retains its power to act upon the declaration, which it did in most cases so far, or not. Thus the power to amend legislation remains with Parliament. Moreover P is not bound by the HRA and retains the power to repeal it when it wishes. Thus PS is preserved.

b) However, it may be argued that PS is challenged in practice. The HRA may nevertheless modify the constitutional arrangement by strengthening the power courts vis a vis Parliament with regards to the substance of laws and thus constitutes of form of entrenchment of its substance. First, the court have a greater power of interpretation and changing the meaning of statutes. In *R v A* Lord **Steyn** established that the interpretation duty placed upon the courts was a strong one and the exercise goes beyond standard interpretation methods. Indeed, the language of the law may be strained to find compatibility and thus the intention of Parliament may be set aside. Also, since the use of Section 4 is a measure of last resort this sets precedent for the courts to use Article 3 and actively engage in interpretation. Second, the HRA renders any inconsistent act practically less effective. Not only could individuals place claims with the ECtHR if they failed to obtain redress with UK courts, also the courts can temporarily suspend the given act via a DOI. Third, According to Thoburn, constitutional statutes may not be subject to implied repeal thus the HRA enjoys some level of entrenchment. Fourth, the HRA allows the courts to establish a body of common law consistent with HR.

Overall we argue that although maintaining PS, the HRA has strengthened the power of the courts vis a vis Parliament. Also, arguably, Parliament has bound itself even prior to the HRA, when the UK party to the Council of Europe became signatory to the European convention on Human Rights and acknowledging the authority of the European Court on Human Rights to rule on such matters. For UK individuals could from that moment place claims with the ECtHR which could formulate rulings inconsistent with UK domestic law.

Devolution

Another challenge to PS is the Devolution and the **Scotland Act 1998** in particular. The orthodox definition of PS implies that the UK Parliament can legislate over all of the UK. The implication of the Devolution Act is that Ireland, Wales and Scotland have legislatures that can make their own legislations I areas devolved to them. Yet any Act passed by these Legislatures could be held invalid in the English courts. **Barnett** argues that in theory, their powers stem from the UK parliament and any Act passed by these legislatures can be repealed by Parliament, much as it could repeal the HRA and the ECA, and those powers could be unilaterally withdrawn by Parliament, thus maintaining the theoretical absolute sovereignty of Parliament. Although PS remains formally intact, we argue that it would be difficult politically, as Lord Denning argued to take back liberties that were granted. It is fair to say that P would face strong opposition if it were to do so.

Jackson

Outside of the EU sphere judges, in Jackson, in obiter, articulated a doctrine of **constitutionalism** which finds its source in common law that has the potential to present a challenge to that of PS. It is significant than the courts were willing to hear a challenge to the legality of an act of Parliament on a non-EU law setting. The issue was whether the Hunting Act, and the Act under which it was made, the Parliament Act 1949, were valid Acts of Parliament. The courts ordinarily have a very limited role to play in deciding such questions. Lord Stein emphasized that PS is a construct of common law and find its source in the courts accepting PS.

This is consistent with **Wade** argument that PS is a made by common law and that what is made by common law could be unmade by common law. Thus it was not unthinkable that PS could be challenged if Parliament did the unthinkable, attempted to curb the power of the courts or significantly limit human rights, for example. Under such circumstances, courts could well not apply unthinkable statutes. The authority for doing so would be the doctrine of the rule of law and human rights, which under such circumstances would be given greater constitutional status that PS. Lord Hope went even further arguing that ultimately the source of PS was the trust the people placed in P. If by doing the unthinkable P were to undermine that trust, there is the possibility that people would question and ultimately reject PS. Judges also raised the notion that P can bind itself by implementing special procedure 'manner and form' thereby binding itself. Although Judges debated PS in obiter, so the views expressed are not law, the very fact that members of the Judiciary debate the contours of PS points to a tension in the constitutional arrangement.

Academic views

Academics have presented different views on the impact of EU developments on PS. **Wade** in his article Sovereignty argues that indeed PS in its Dicean definition has been eroded. When enacting the 1972 Act, P has effectively bound future P and since Factortame, 'a revolution', the courts have contributed to eroding PS. **Barber** argues that PS rule was abandoned in the pivotal case of Factortame. Nevertheless, Parliamentary sovereignty which definition has changed enjoys an emotional pull among scholars has it shaped the constitutional arrangement in the UK. He considers that the focus of analysis should be the vitality of Parliament as an institution within the constitutional arrangement. Baroness **Hale** in *Jackson* argues that 'Parliament has limited its own power, for now'

Bognador argues that the constitutional arrangement in the UK relies on some higher pre-existing rule i.e. the rule of law. On the other hand, **Craig** argues that PS remains intact because P has itself set limits to its sovereignty and still has the power to modify those limits. The role of the courts may have changed but they have not played a significant role in imposing limits on P. Lord **Neuberger**, commenting on Jackson also considers that the courts acted on the basis, not of absolute rights but on the basis of rights granted to them by Parliament. Thus PS is intact.

McCormick, providing a political analysis argues that in today's world, the economic benefits attached to some limitation of sovereignty far outweigh the benefits of absolute sovereignty. It is thus not realistic to seek absolute sovereignty.

Overall, Political constitutionalists consider that Parliament legitimizes laws. Politicians should have the ultimate power. Elections and in between the confidence of parliament ensures the views of the majority is decisive. They support majoritarism in democracy. At some point in history they distrusted courts for having a conservative political agenda.

However, Legal constitutionalists view courts and enforceable rights are key to creating conditions under which government power is limited. They reject the notion of majoritarism. Parliamentary control of government is seen as ineffective. Government controls Parliament and thus PS is too weak to curb government. It provides no guarantee to fundamental rights. Principles such as the rule of law should be the most important principle of the constitution.

We argue that Parliament bound itself as a result of the UK willingly joining the EU, but it may change its position at any time if the political circumstances allow for it. Also, the balance of power between courts and Parliament may well evolve over time and further erode PS.

Essay Question 2

As time has passed Dicey's account of Parliamentary sovereignty has become increasingly difficult to reconcile with constitutional reality in the UK. Critically discuss this statement.

Answer

Introduction

A.V. Dicey's definition of parliamentary supremacy, which has lost validity as quoted above, will be analysed critically. First this paper will examine the doctrine of parliamentary supremacy as laid down by Dicey. Second this study will examine how European case law has taken precedents over English law and how the United Kingdom courts have dealt with this. Third this study will present arguments advanced by academics. Forth this study will examine the relationship between the Human Rights Act ("HRA") 1998 and Parliament's sovereignty. In particular it will look at the functioning of section 3 and 4 and parliamentary sovereignty. Lastly this paper will conclude its findings.

Definition of Parliamentary Supremacy

A.V. Dicey said 127 years ago that the principle of Parliamentary sovereignty was: that Parliament has the right to make or unmake any law. Moreover, no person or body is recognized by the law of England as having a right to override or set aside legislation. Second Parliament cannot bind its successors.[62]

Membership to the EU

The doctrine of Parliamentary supremacy holds that the Parliament is the supreme legislature. Nevertheless, the European Court of Justice ("ECJ") has asserted the Supremacy of EU law over and above national law. In a famous EU law case the ECJ sated *obita* that the UK had limited its Sovereignty in certain areas, when signing the Treaty which allowed them to enter the EU.[63] The

---

[62] Dicey AV, Introduction to the Study of the Law of the Constitution (1885), 10th ed, 1959, London: Macmillan at p. 39

court in <u>Costa v ENEL</u>[64] stated that the EC Treaty *"carries with it a clear limitation of sovereign rights"*.[65] The crucial issue of whether EU regulations take precedence over UK's was explored by a court in <u>Internationale Handelgesellschaft v EVCF</u>.[66] There has been a different conception of the issue between the UK and the EU. The ECJ predicated that *'The Law borne from the treaty cannot have the courts opposing it with rules of national law of any nature whatsoever...'.* In the <u>Costa</u> case, the ECJ said that national laws could be pre-empted either prior or subsequent to the enactment of community legislation, which has been enacted in the <u>European Communities Act ("ECA") 1972</u>.

The ECA 1972

Section 2(1) of the ECA says that EC treaties and law will have direct applicability in the UK. This gives primacy to the EU law. This has lead to confusion in the UK courts as there have been a number of occasions where EU law and Acts of Parliament conflict and individuals who rely on the treaty may debate that the treaty must be given effect under the ECA 1972.

UK case law

UK case law is not conclusive with how far Parliamentary Supremacy goes with regard to the EU. Lord Denning in <u>Macarthy's v. Smith</u>[67] stated that European law is a method of statutory interpretation or an aid to construction. In this case Cumming Bruce LJ, disagreed with his approach that held if Community law is clear it should bypass national law, more in accordance with direct effect approach in <u>Van Gen Loss</u> and <u>Costa</u>.[68] However, the House of Lords seems to have clarified the law now in <u>R v Secretary of State for Transport ex p Factortame</u>.[69]

---

[63] Van Gend En Loos, Case 26/62; Costa v ENEL, Case 6/64; Simmenthal, Case 106/77.
[64] Case 6/64 (15 July 1964)
[65] *Ibid.*
[66] 11/70 [1970] ECR 1125
[67] [1979] 3 All ER 325
[68] Ibid per Lord Justice Cumming Bruce
[69] (No.2) [1991] 1 All ER 70, HL

Factortame

In response to the case Factortame, the UK Parliament enacted the Merchant Shipping Act 1988 which conflicted with EC law which allows the freedom to set up and operate companies everywhere in the European Union. The Spanish companies then argued that EC law is supposed to prevail over and asked for an interim injunction against the 1988 Act. The House of Lords thereupon granted an order restraining the Secretary of State from enforcing the legislation.

Academic Opinion

This effects Dicey's definition of Parliamentary Sovereignty, as the courts set the Merchant Shipping Act aside. William Wade's in his article 'Sovereignty – Revolution or Evolution?' regarded this as revolutionary. He claimed a loss of absolute sovereignty, because this has never been seen before in our constitutional arrangement.[70] Another way to see this issue is presented by Craig and De Burca, who argue supremacy remains intact and courts role has changed by letting Parliament set limits to their supremacy, so in that sense that Parliament has restricted itself too by enacting the ECA and courts should respect that.[71] Nevertheless, there is another argument by N. MacCormick who thinks that in today's time Parliamentary Sovereignty cannot exist in such a way presented by Dicey due to interdependence of economies. [72]

Moreover, the doctrine of Implied repeal states that *"where two acts conflict, the more recent prevails"*[73] (which has been the matter in Thoburn v Sunderland County Council[74],) this is supported by Dicey's approach saying that Parliament cannot bind its successors. What can be argued is the s. 2(4) ECA 1972

---

[70] Wade, W, 'Sovereignty – Revolution or Evolution?' (1996) 112 LQR 568
[71] Paul Craig / Gráinne de Búrca, EU Law, 3rd ed., 2003, 301-312
72 N. MacCormick, Questioning Sovereignty, (1999), OUP, p.117-121
[73] Elliot M, Parliamentary Sovereignty under pressure, International Journal of Constitutional Law, 2004 at page 550
[74] (2002) Times 22/2/02, DC

suspends the doctrine of implied repeal. Laws LJ stated that EU law prevails over an Act of Parliament and as the 1972 Act is a constitutional statute, it can only be repealed with the express intention of Parliament.

It can be argued the 'classical Dician doctrine' is not eroded by Factortame. For example it can be argued Parliament has not lost its Parliamentary Supremacy, it is just not using it, similar to what Craig and DeBurca are asserting. Nevertheless, Laws LJ explained this by saying that Dicey's definition (being 127 years old) is valid but has been modified by case law such as Factortame.

On the other hand, Lord Denning, obviously without knowledge of Factortame, argued in Bulmer v Bollinger[75] that *"no longer is European Law an incoming tide flowing up the estuaries of England. It is now like a tidal wave bringing down our sea walls and flowing inland over our fields and houses – to the dismay of all".* [76] in response to this an exaggerated perception was offered by Seamus Burnes, who said Lord Denning *"might have to revise his image of EU law being like an incoming tide permeating our existing legal order, and more realistically compare it to a tsunami enveloping everything in its path with irresistible force."*.[77]

Conclusion

In conclusion, Dicey's definition has been encroached upon because of the case of **Factortame** and the House of Lords was quite prepared to set aside the Merchant Shipping Act 1998. Furthermore, the fact that Parliament cannot bind its successors has also been violated because of section 2(4) ECA 1972 which has the effect of suspending the doctrine of implied repeal.

---

[75] [1974] 2 All ER 1226
[76] The Independent, 16th July 1996
[77] Seamus Burns, An incoming tide [2008] 158 NLJ 44

Chapter 7 - The Crown and the Prerogative

Essay Question 1

Can courts can ensure that those using prerogative powers remain accountable. Discuss?

Answer

Introduction

Many legislative and administrative powers have been enjoyed by governments throughout history under the banner of powers that fall under the 'royal prerogative'. It has been described by many as an 'anachronism of the constitution' and in need of reform.[78] This paper shall briefly outline the problem areas that arise from the operation of such prerogative powers, what has been done till date to address these problems and what more, either by way of legislation or active judicial scrutiny, can be done to reform the operation of the prerogative.

Royal prerogatives

A.V Dicey perhaps gave the most easily comprehensible definition of prerogative powers; he said *"...the residue of discretionary or arbitrary authority, which at any time is legally left in the hands of the Crown ...Every act which the executive government can lawfully do without the authority of an Act of Parliament is done in virtue of this prerogative."*[79] The problem with royal prerogatives as described in the statement is that there is a 'democratic deficit' in the exercise of these powers. Cohn says *"Government action in the absence of statutory authorisation is an anomaly, as it runs contrary to basic democratic principles."*[80]

---

[78] Markesinis, B. S. (1973). The Royal Prerogative Re-Visited. The Cambridge Law Journal, 32(02), 287-309.
[79] Barnett, H. (2014), *Constitutional & administrative law*, Routledge
[80] Margit Cohn, 'Judicial Review of non-statutory executive powers after Bancoult: a unified anxious model', Public Law 2009, Apr, 260-286

For instance consider the prerogative to dissolve parliament. Under this prerogative it was the Crown that could dissolve Parliament on its own proposal. In modern times, the Crown would however not do such without the advice of her ministers. While this absolves the Crown from political embarrassment it creates a problem within the operation of the prerogative and since 1918 the prerogative operated under the convention that the Crown shall dissolve Parliament at the request of the Prime Minister.[81] Therefore, the timing of an election and logically the duration of a government remained within the discretion of the Prime Minister. It might seem odd to many that, in a democracy, a matter as important as the calling of the election and dissolution of Parliament remains within the hands of the executive and not the elected Parliament. Not only so, the Prime Minister is not even required to consult Parliament on this matter. Recent changes in legislation which have brought an end to this particular prerogative power[82] but only go towards highlighting the need for reform.

Prerogative and Statute

The general principle, in conformity with the doctrine of Parliamentary Sovereignty, is that Parliament has the power and the right to restrict, preserve or abolish prerogative powers. In *Attorney General V de Keyser's Royal Hotel Ltd,*[83] the government sought to bypass the Defence of the Realm Act 1914, by seeking to rely on a prerogative which governed the same matter as the statute. The court held that the government was unable to rely on the prerogative power as there was an Act of Parliament on the same matter.

Judicial Control of prerogatives

Here the problem that we face concerns the extent to which the

---

[81] Newman, W. J. (2009). Of Dissolution, Prorogation, and Constitutional Law, Principle and Convention: Maintaining Fundamental Distinctions During a Parliamentary Crisis. National Journal of Constitutional Law, 27, 217.
[82] The Fixed-term Parliaments Act 2011, places the dissolution of Parliament and calling of elections on a statutory basis.
[83] [1920] AC 508, HL(E)

courts are willing to review the scope and exercise of these far reaching non-statutory powers. In *R v Criminal Injuries Compensation Board ex parte Lain*[84] it was made clear that the Board had been created under a prerogative rather than a statute and this did not mean that it was not amenable to judicial review. However, while accepting that prerogatives can be judicially reviewed, the courts nevertheless reside within the bounds of a self imposed restriction on which prerogatives they ought not to review. In the GCHQ case it was held by Lord Roskill that matters such as *"the appointment of ministers, dissolution of Parliament, grant of honours, treaties and matters of national security"*, were matters of high policy and therefore, not appropriate subject matters to be reviewed by the courts. [85]

Similarly, the courts also restrict themselves, when it comes to the extent of review that is possible of prerogative powers. In *R v (Bancoult) v Secretary of State for Foreign and Commonwealth Affairs (No 2)*,[86] the House Lords decided that in principle a prerogative Order in Council can be subject to ordinary grounds of judicial review. However, this approach does not take into account that it is difficult to apply the ordinary principles of judicial review to prerogatives. This is because in an ordinary judicial review the court will ascertain the proper limits of a decision maker's act by understanding the relevant statute. However, in the case of prerogative power there is no governing statute to deliberate.[87] Therefore, the approach fails to take into account the democratic deficit in these powers and as a result fail to satisfactorily scrutinise their use.

Reforms

The first reform is to bring the prerogative under statutory control. In recent years we have seen that prerogative powers such as Dissolution of Parliament and Resignation of Government

---

[84] [1967] 2 QB 864
[85] *Council of Civil Service Unions v Minister for the Civil Service* [1983] UKHL 6
[86] [2008] UKHL 61
[87] Richard Moules, 'Judicial Review of prerogative Orders in Council', Cambridge Law Journal 2009, 68(1), 14-17.

following a loss of confidence vote have been brought under statutory control by the enactment of the Fixed –Term Parliaments Act 2011. This is an improvement as any executive power exercised under the statute can be review under ordinary principles of judicial review. Further, the Constitutional Reform and Governance Act 2010 has placed the regulation of the civil service on a statutory footing for the first time.

The second method, of controlling the use of prerogative powers, in the absence of statutory reform would be to introduce a stricter criterion of judicial review. Margit Cohn, suggests a model. First a legal system should prohibit non-statutory action that directly affects human rights and freedoms. Second the rule of residually, according to which existence of statute excludes non-statutory action in the same subject-matter, should be firmly followed. Third such powers should be assessed by a loose pro-legislation rule, under which issues that have long-lasting bearing on society, should generally be treated as requiring statute[88].

Conclusion

In conclusion, from the above discussion we have seen that prerogatives pose significant problems in the area of its scope, its relationship with statutes and the control that has been exercised by the courts. By introducing a stricter and careful review process, over and above judicial review, the courts can ensure that those using such powers remain accountable.

---

[88] Margit Cohn, 'Judicial Review of non-statutory executive powers after Bancoult: a unified anxious model', Public Law 2009, Apr, 260-286

Chapter 8 - Powers and accountability of the executive

Question Essay 1

'Identify the constitutional powers of a Prime Minister of the UK and examine how effectively he or she may be made responsible for the government's decisions and actions.' Dicuss.

Answer

Introduction

The purpose of this essay is to discuss the constitutional powers of the Prime Minister (hereinafter 'PM') and to examine how accountable he or she could be made for the government's actions and decisions. It is important at this point to provide a historical background in pursuance of an examination of the existing legal status of the PM's office. This essay will focus on some basic components of the constitution including collective ministerial responsibility as well as judicial review of the actions of the PM. As a final point, there will be an examination of the separation of powers in view of the role of the PM, in constitutional reform. It will conclude with an evaluation of the significance of the PM's office relative to the constitution.

Background

The UK[89] constitution is mostly unwritten[90]. It is mainly comprised of conventional practices evolved from the middle ages. The PM's office has emerged under such conventions, partially from practice, the royal prerogative, custom as well as the 'nods and winks' from the party leadership position but most especially it has been integrated by statutes in contemporary history.[91] The Monarch appoints the PM, who in theory has the authority to appoint and dismiss the PM under the royal prerogative. [92] The

---

[89] Often incorrectly referred to as the "English constititution".
[90] FF Ridley, 'There is no British Constitution: A dangerous Case of the Emperor's Clothes' in *Parliamentary Affairs* (1988) 41(3), pp 340-361.
[91] J Alder, *Constitutional and Administrative Law*, 7th ed. (Hampshire, Palgrave MacMillan 2009) pp 281-283.

Monarch is not elected and is therefore not accountable to the electorate. [93] The PM's office carries out functions in the Monarch's name.[94] According to the convention the leader of the political party in power is the PM. the political party comes to power with the majority of votes (on its own or with a coalition) won in an election. [95] The Monarch has discretion to choose who to consult when the PM resigns, retires or passes away whilst being in office even though at first it would be appropriate to find consensus between the senior members of the majority party. [96] Ever since the beginning of the 20th century, 10 out of the 25 PMs have come into power from a general election, the rest were chosen privately from the arrangements of the party.[97]

Functions of the office of PM

Although the Monarch has executive powers in the UK, it is the PM and his or her government who perform executive functions in the name of the Crown. Prerogative powers are passed in a similar way as well. Traditionally, the Crown reigns, however the PM and his Cabinet ministers rule.[98] The PM's office functions' are wide; from being accountable for overall security, managing the civil service to sending armed forces to sensitive political regions in accordance to statutes such as the Intelligence Services Act 1994, Police Act 1997, National Audit Act 1983, National Minimum Wages Act 1998.[99] Lately, the PM has taken control over foreign policy which is a perfect illustration of convention-making in practice.[100]

---

[92] Heffernan, R. (2005). Exploring (and explaining) the British prime minister. The British Journal of Politics & International Relations, 7(4), 605-620

[93] H Barnett, *Constitutional & Administrative Law*, 7th ed. (London, Routledge-Cavendish 2009) p 13.

[94] Ibid

[95] Ibid, p 118.

[96] Alder (note 3) p 282.

[97] Ibid, p 281.

[98] See DirectGov, *Central Government, Citizens and Rights*, available online at:
<http://www.direct.gov.uk/en/Governmentcitizensandrights/UKgovernment/Centralgovernmentandthemonarchy/DG_073442>.

[99] Alder, (note 3) p 282.

The Office of PM and separation of powers

Parliament is the critical legal aspect of the PM's office in the constitution. The Dicean doctrine of Parliamentary sovereignty suggests that under the British constitution, Parliament has the power to make or unmake any law whatever.[101] However, in reality Parliament is weak since the government in power dominates it. [102] Furthermore, the courts continue to be subject to Parliament. The executive's position (controlled by the PM) is harder to ascertain since it is a part of the Parliament. The PM as well as the Cabinet, are considered members of the Parliament and it is there where they discuss policies and make decisions.[103] Therefore it can be seen that when a PM has a majority in Parliament, he is 'Parliament' and thus has the power to implement any constitutional reform he pleases. This contradicts Montesquieu's doctrine of separation of powers.[104]

In the 19th century Bagehot stated that there are obvious benefits to a constitution with a separation of powers. He perceived the close relationship among Parliament and the executive as an illustration of 'the efficient secret of the English constitution' and described it as 'the close union, the nearly complete fusion, of the executive and legislative powers' although he recognised it was not as good as one would think it would from the books. [105] Nonetheless, this view is not accepted because in the present electoral process which brings about a government with a majority of seats in Parliament, amounts to an 'elective dictatorship'. [106] Barnett argues that Bagehot's view is an oversimplified and incorrect depiction of how the constitution works. [107]

---

[100] Ibid.
[101] AV Dicey, *The Law of the Constitution*, 10th ed. (1965), pp 39-40.
[102] Alder (note 3) pp 147-148.
[103] M Allen and B Thompson, Cases and Materials on Constitutional & Administrative Law, 7th ed. (Oxford UK, OUP 2002) pp 267-270.
[104] Barnett (note 4) p 88.
[105] W Bagehot, *The English Constitution 1891*, (London, Collins, 1963 reprint) pp 67-68.
[106] Lord Hailsham in (1976) 120 SJ 93 cited via Barnett (note 4) p 88.
[107] Ibid.

The Office of PM in practice

In accordance to convention and custom, the PM who is the head of the government is naturally the leader of the majority in the House of Commons. A coalition government is set up if there is no political party that has more than half the seats. This was the case with the 2010 government. If not, one vote would be critical to determine a majority as was the case with Margaret Thatcher. All of the PM's powers derive from the convention;[108] only few are conferred to by law. Those legal powers deriving from convention and custom are the most important. [109] Theoretically, the Crown appoints and removes ministers. Conventionally though, the Crown takes action upon the advice of the PM, thus suggesting that in reality the PM has the real power. Furthermore, the PM appoints various significant public posts which have originated from statutory powers as well as the convention. Moreover, the PM has exclusive power to decide what the agenda of the Cabinet is and when it meets. Essentially, the PM has full control of the government since he controls the Cabinet and the party whips in Parliament. [110]

Accountability

The PM's powers are scrutinised through collective ministerial responsibility. It is also a conventional practice where the PM and his Cabinet are collectively responsible to the House of Commons that have the power to give a vote of 'no confidence'. If this is the case then they must resign. Theoretically, the Crown is authorised to dismiss the PM, however custom states that the PM should submit his resignation or must request from the Monarch to dissolve Parliament. [111] Nevertheless, the strengths of the PM and the opposition govern the capacity to defeat a vote of confidence in the House of Commons. If there is a strong government with a majority it will most likely not succeed. However, when there is a coalition government, the outcome is uncertain since neither party

---

[108] Similar to PM's office
[109] Alder (note 3) pp 281-285.
[110] Ibid, p 282.
[111] Allen and Thompson (note 12) pp 271-303.

has a majority. James Callaghan was the last PM to lose a vote of confidence and as a result had to resign which called for an early election.[112] However, it must be emphasised that this is a convention thus a political measure will be enforced only in extreme situations and it does not carry legal importance. Collective ministerial responsibility includes confidentiality of Cabinet meeting minutes which reflects a pragmatic business practice.[113]

Further restrictions, checks and balances are mainly political that have minimal legal effect therefore are not important for constitutional purposes. The Crown has the authority to interfere in grave circumstances including dissolution of Parliament, appointing a PM in a constitutional crisis and appointing peers.[114] Party considerations could restrain the power of the PM to a certain extent as he or she could depend on the Cabinet's support. Any PM could be removed from being a party leader as was the case with Margaret Thatcher in 1989. Theoretically, the Monarch could reject any attempt from the PM to dissolve Parliament. Provided that the office of the PM is not a distinct department even though it is a Private Office; he or she has special advisors who have executive powers.[115]

The opposition has an important role due to the fact that it checks that the PM's office carries out its constitutional duties efficiently, through suggestions of alternative policies and solutions, and just by simply opposing and challenging the PM and his government.[116]

Even though there are constitutional problems in the relationship between the PM/government and Parliament, Parliament can still restrain the power of the PM's to legislate. It would be unrealistic to assume that the government can pass all legislation. An illustration would be the 1983-4 Police and Criminal Evidence Bill that was amended significantly due to pressure received from all political parties, academics, pressure groups as well as lawyers.[117]

---

[112] Barnett (note 4) p 88.
[113] Allend and Thompson (note 12) pp 271-303.
[114] Alder (note 3) pp 263-278.
[115] Alder (note 3) p 283.
[116] Barnett (note 4) p 89.

However, it must be emphasised that this establishes parts of the political ways of checking and balancing without having carrying any importance on the legal constitutional rules.

Removal

The only formal ways to remove a PM is by intervention from the Monarch[118] or by impeachment from the Parliament which leads to his/her removal by the party.

Judicial Review of PM acts

As seen previously, the PM's office theoretically enjoys too much practice and there is not much in place that keeps it in check efficiently. Nevertheless, there are certain principles in the UK uncodified constitution that limits the possibility of a tyrannical PM. in accordance with the rule of law the executive officials are not able to exercise power unless authorised by a legal rule. [119] However, it is important to note that the PM's acts are reviewable. In *Council of Civil Service Unions v Minister for Civil Service* (1985)[120] the House of Lords stated that jurisdiction over holdings of executive power making decisions authorised from prerogative powers are reviewable in a similar way to decisions made from statutory powers. Nevertheless, the courts will not always exercise this power of review. There must be justiciable power, in other words, it must be appropriate for scrutiny of the courts, thus will be looking at the suitability with regards to the case facts and the subject matter. In *R (Gentle) v Prime Minister and others* (2008)[121], the claim that Article 2 of the ECHR calls for a governmental inquiry into the invasion of Iraq was rejected.

Finally, there are no legal instruments that inhibit the incumbent of the PM's office from restricting judicial review even though the courts are given inferiority. An important question posed by Lord Woolf is 'what happens if a party with a large majority in Parliament uses that majority to abolish the courts' entire power of

---

[117] Ibid.
[118] Not very likely but could happen theoretically
[119] Allen and Thompson (note 12) p 174.
[120] AC 374.
[121] UKHL 20.

judicial review'?[122] In theory, a party with a majority could act upon this. So far, the only obstacle to the PM powers, are the political checks and balances that do not have anything strictly legal or constitutional which prevents a tyrannical rule by a PM. however, these have made the UK one of the most efficient liberal democracies in the world.

Conclusion

Therefore it can be seen, that the PM's office is a vital institution of the constitutional system in the UK. He or she acts as a mediator between the Monarch and Parliament, which makes this role highly important for the constitution. The most important part of the role is the proposing and carrying out legislative reforms that directly affect the constitution. Here the power of the PM's office is restricted by collective ministerial responsibility. Generally, the PM has a wide range of powers with little or no means to scrutinise him/her. The majority of these powers are based on convention. Political tools remain as the only form of balancing. Even though there are several flaws in the system, the way it works currently and the potential abuse warned by Montesquieu, has never taken place in the UK.

Essay question 2

Evaluate the extent to which constitutional conventions are able to provide any effective protection against the excesses of executive power.

Answer

Firstly, in order to provide an adequate evaluation, 'constitutional conventions' and the 'executive' must be defined. The 'executive' can be described as the section of the state that creates policy and is responsible for the operation of those policies (Barnett, 2002). Therefore in formal terms the sovereign is the head of the executive although in practice this position lies primarily with the

---

[122] Lord Woolf of Barnes, 'Droit public- English Style' [1995] *Public Law* 57.

Prime Minister, his cabinet, and other ministers, followed by those in the Police and the armed forces. Whilst most countries have a written constitution to define the rules, regulations and practices of an executive, Britain (along with Israel and New Zealand) has no such document. It thus follows that formal protections against the exercise of power which exist in those countries with a written constitution do not exist in Britain (Bradley and Ewing, 2003). Instead, the British constitution has three sources of rules: Acts of Parliament; judicial precedent; and non-legal rules known as constitutional conventions, (Allen and Thompson, 2002). A.V. Dicey (1965) defines constitutional conventions as:

> "...understandings, habits or practices which, though they may regulate the conduct of the several members of the sovereign power, of the Ministry, or of other officials, are not in reality laws at all since they are not enforced by the courts." (as cited in Carroll, 2002: 51).

Since these conventions are not written down and are unenforceable through a court of law, the question of their effectiveness arises. The following discussion aims to consider how such a phenomenon has the ability to control discretion and monopolisation of power (or if indeed it does at all), and why apparently unenforceable rules are observed by those working within the constitution.

Bradley and Wade (1990) point out that under every system of government, whether it has a written constitution or not, non-legal rules will develop. However, they are especially significant in Britain since it is through such rules that a cabinet government has developed. As discussed by Wade (1965), there is no legal obligation for Ministers to consult committees which now play such an important role in the policy making process. Indeed, it is noted that the government could not function effectively without such a system of committees, although there is no legal requirement for them. As the purpose of the system is to ensure harmony between the Government and the public (Wade, 1965), it could be argued that this particular convention illustrates one of the ways in which informal rules act as effective protection from the excess of executive power since proposals are discussed in cabinet committees and arguments of objection may be made.

In contrast however, ministers may find themselves bound by decisions in which they have had little involvement due to an increasing network of committees (Hogan, 2000). Moreover, the amount of power the Prime Minister has can be illustrated by the conventions surrounding the cabinet and committees. Such practices include the Prime

Minister appointing and dismissing government ministers, deciding how tasks should be allocated to departments and whether new departments should be created and existing ones abolished, and being in control of what issues are to be discussed hence effectively controlling the whole decision making process (Bradley and Ewing, 2003). Additionally, once a decision has been made, all members of the government, cabinet members or otherwise, are bound to support it, even though rather than a vote on issues, the Prime Minister merely takes a sense of the meeting. Furthermore, it is noted by Bradley and Ewing (2003):

> *"...that many decisions of government are not taken by the cabinet as a whole, but by the Prime minister in consultation with a few colleagues."* (Bradley and Ewing, 2003: 262).

Significantly, if ministers feel they strongly object to a final decision, by convention they should resign (Hogan, 2000). This can be illustrated by the resignation of the Defence Secretary, Michael Heseltine, during the Westland Affair 1986. According to a BBC article Heseltine felt he had no alternative but to resign from Margaret Thatcher's Cabinet since his views on the future of the Westland helicopter company were being ignored. Moreover, once again illustrating the powers of the Prime Minister, Mrs Thatcher sustained that all Heseltine's public opinions on the matter should be vetted by officials before being released. It could be argued that in these circumstances, the constitutional convention of collective responsibility does not provide effective protection against excessive executive power since a minority in strong opposition who may represent a significant number of the public are by convention, required to resign.

It is a significant nature of constitutional conventions that because they are not enforced through the law that they can be changed to suit the needs of a government or suspended when they are inconvenient. In relation to collective responsibility, the convention was formally but temporarily stopped during the campaign preceding the referendum on the continuation of EU membership (Hogan, 2000). An example of disregarding conventions can be shown by the Southern Rhodesia Act brought in by Parliament in 1965. Although it was the convention that Parliament should not legislate for a dominion unless requested by the dominion concerned, Parliament proceeded to respond to Rhodesia's declaration of independence by declaring that it remained a British dominion and proclaimed its legislation invalid, (Carroll, 2002). Significantly, in the case of *Madzimbamuto* v *Lardner-Burke* [1969] 1 AC 645 the Privy Council refused to accept arguments that the 1965 Act should not be applied because it was in breach of a convention (Carroll, 2002). Lord Reid, speaking for the Privy Council, said that although the convention was a very important one, it had no legal limitations on the power of Parliament. He continued with:

> *"It is often said that it would be unconstitutional for United Kingdom Parliament to do such things…But that does not mean it is beyond the power of Parliament to do such things. If Parliament*

> *chose to do any of them the Courts could not hold the Act of Parliament invalid."* (as cited in Allen and Thompson, 2002: 247)

This strongly suggests that conventions are not effective in limiting the powers of the executive. One way in which it could be argued that constitutional conventions do provide effective protection against the monopolisation of executive power could be the diminished role of the sovereign. The role of the sovereign in the organisation of the government has almost disappeared since the eighteenth century. For example, the last time a Royal Assent

Bill was refused was by the Queen in 1708 (Bradley and Wade, 1990). The Queen is formally the head of the executive and all Acts of Parliament are technically enacted by the Queen who has the legal right to refuse to give the royal assent to Bills passed by both the House of Commons and Lords (Barnett, 2002). Nevertheless, by convention, the Queen does not have the power to refuse laws passed by the majority of Parliament: by convention she must assent to Bills unless she is otherwise advised by the government. Political power traditionally exercised by the monarch therefore has been transferred to the government. This is acknowledged by Wheare (1966) who describes that one of the ways in which conventions affect the law of the constitution is that power is transferred from one person to another. Importantly, although this may appear to have effectively taken considerable political powers from the hands of one individual, it could be argued that there has been a complete transfer of power from the monarch to the Prime Minister as suggested by Hogan (2000):

> *"...in practice we now have a constitutional monarchy where the Queen acts on the advice of her Prime Minister."* (Hogan, 2000: 3).

When discussing constitutional conventions and the power vested in the executive, the doctrine of the separation of powers is of significant importance. It was noted by Montesquieu, a French jurist in the eighteenth century that the three functions of government: the legislative, executive and the judicial, must be exercised by entirely different bodies and that there should be no overlap of function (Carroll, 2002: Hogan, 2000). Montesquieu argued that if any overlap should occur, this would lead to tyranny. Although various conventions do exist to attempt to keep a separation of powers in Britain, such as lay members in the House of Lords prohibited from participating in its judicial functions (Carroll, 2002), and that judges shall not play an active role in political life, there are not sufficient rules to prevent overlap. For example, the Lord Chancellor is a member of all three branches of the government (Hogan, 2000). Perhaps if Britain had a written constitution like the United States of America, there would be a clearer separation of powers based on written rules rather than conventions, ensuring no monopolisation of power could occur.

Indeed, the monopolisation of power by the Prime Minister is a major concern of Lord Hailsham in his "Elective Dictatorship" report. He proposes that because Britain imposes no limitations on the government, the Powers of Parliament are unlimited. Referring to constitutional conventions as limitations to the power of Parliament Lord Hailsham continues:

> *"The limitations on it, are only political and moral. They are found in the consciences of members, in the necessity for periodical elections, and in the so called checks and balances..."* (as cited in a BBC document).

The only limitations given by conventions therefore according to Lord Hailsham are the consciences of the ministers, and the hope for re-election. He continues to describe how the government now controls Parliament rather than Parliament controlling the government, since discussions used to influence how members voted, but now he suggests it has become convention for members to be persuaded through the 'whip' system. This means that members are persuaded through fear of dismissal or no movement from the back bench to other positions. Therefore, Lord Hailsham concluded that Britain is ruled under an elective dictatorship. Conventions thus do not appear to provide protection against executive power.

In contrast to Lord Hailsham's views that conventions are only followed due to the conscience of ministers and the hope for re-election is the case of Attorney General v Jonathon Cape Ltd [1976] QB 752 which involved the political diary of Richard Crossman written while he was a Cabinet minister. After his death the diary was edited for publication, although because of the detailed accounts of discussions at Cabinet

meetings, the Secretary to the Cabinet refused to have it published. After the publication went ahead, the Attorney-General sought an injunction to stop it (Carroll, 2002). The judiciary recognised the convention of collective responsibility, although it is noted by Bradley and Ewing (2003) that it was only one of many factors taken into account in establishing the limits of the doctrine of confidence. Nevertheless, this case does show that the judiciary will recognise conventions *"as a matter of practical reality"*, (Molan, 2004: 2). This strengthens the argument that constitutional conventions provide protection against excessive executive power.

Another contradiction to Lord Hailsham's "Elective Dictatorship" report could be the conventional rule that the government must have the confidence of the majority in the Commons (Bradley and Ewing, 2003). If not, the government is said to have lost the vote of confidence and must either resign or seek a dissolution of Parliament from the Queen (Barnett, 2002). Moreover, this situation is cited by Lee and Stallworthy (1995) as giving back benchers a chance to express their disproval without necessarily putting their political life at risk as suggested by Lord Hailsham. By convention therefore, powers in the hand of the Prime Minister and his government are controlled since a majority vote in the House of Commons must be achieved by the government in order to remain in power.

A further convention which appears to keep a check on the conduct and discretion of the government is the meeting of Parliament. As suggested by Carroll (2002), the Parliament should constantly supervise the executive. Although there is a legal requirement for Parliament to meet 'frequently' under the Bill of Rights (1689), and at least once every three years under the Meeting of Parliament Act (1694), Carroll (2002) points that such legal requirements are insufficient in controlling the activities of the executive. Therefore, it is the constitutional convention that Parliament should be summoned annually which helps provide protection against an excess of executive power.

- When evaluating the information presented it is clear that there is evidence to support both sides of the argument as to whether constitutional conventions provide any effective protection against the excess of executive power. Moreover, there are debates as to why conventions are followed and whether or not Britain requires a written constitution to limit the power of the executive. It could be suggested that an advantage of having informal rules and conventions surrounding the Monarchy is that the

Queen still remains to hold some legal powers, although she does not use them. For this reason, the Monarchy continues to survive in Britain which aids the economy through tourism. Regarding powers of the executive, conventions are met with speculation from those who draw on the unenforceability of such rules through the law such as Lord Hailsham (as discussed above). However, it should be noted that conventions give the British constitution an essential degree of flexibility, allowing it to change, develop and adapt to contemporary society without having to alter many existing legal rules (Carroll, 2002).

Nevertheless, it is argued that such flexibility is for some a cause for concern since it allows governments to amend rules in its favour as illustrated by *Madzimbamuto* v *Lardner-Burke* [1969] 1 AC 645 (see above). Additionally, the arguments that we are beginning to see the rise of an elective dictatorship in Britain also cast doubt on the effectiveness of constitutional conventions. However I think it is important to remember that, and as noted by Hogan (2000), the Prime Minister's strength largely depends on the support of his party both inside and outside Parliament. Thatcher's downfall in 1990 demonstrates the ultimate dependence on party support. This is supported by Sir Ivor Jennings' statement in his "Cabinet Government": conventions *"not only are followed, but have to be followed"*, (as cited in Barnett, 2002). When considering this in addition to no confidence votes, the regular meeting of Parliament and evident judicial recognition of non-legal practices, it cannot be assumed that the Prime Minister has ultimate power, and can be concluded that constitutional conventions provide at least some effective protection against the excess of executive power.

Chapter 9 – The Decentralisation of public powers

Essay question 1

What is devolution? Discuss.

Answer

Devolution is the process of devolving power from the centre to sub-national units. It is different from a federal system of government, since under the doctrine of parliamentary sovereignty devolution is in theory reversible and the devolved institutions are constitutionally subordinate to the UK Parliament. The legislative framework for devolution is set out in the *Scotland Act 1998,* the *Government of Wales Act 1998* and the *Northern Ireland Act 1998.* There is also a non-legislative framework of concordats, agreements between Government departments and the devolved institutions, under a *Memorandum of Understanding.*

Scotland

The UK system of devolution is asymmetric, in that there are different levels of devolved responsibilities and there is no common pattern. Scotland, Wales and Northern Ireland all have different forms of devolution. Scotland has a Parliament and an Executive developed from the Westminster model. Under the *Scotland Act 1998,* the Parliament can pass Acts and the Executive can make secondary legislation in areas other than those which are reserved to Westminster. Committees are central to the working of the Parliament. They combine scrutiny of the Executive and of legislation. In addition, the Parliament has the power to vary the standard rate of income tax by up to 3 percentage points from the UK level, although it has not yet used this power. The Westminster Parliament can legislate in devolved areas, but under the Sewel Convention, will only do so, if asked by the Scottish Parliament.

Wales

Under the *Government of Wales Act 1998*, powers in devolved areas which used to be exercised by UK ministers have been delegated to the National Assembly for Wales as a single corporate body. Therefore in law there is no separate executive and legislature, but in practice the Assembly has moved towards a separation of legislative and executive functions within the constraints of the Act. The Assembly can make delegated or secondary legislation, such as orders and regulations, in devolved areas, but primary legislation for Wales in devolved areas is still made by the UK Parliament.

Northern Ireland

The progress of devolution in Northern Ireland is inextricably bound up with the peace process, and problems with this have led to the Assembly and Executive being suspended four times, most recently since October 2002. When functioning the
Northern Ireland Assembly can make primary and delegated legislation in those areas which are transferred. The UK Parliament legislates in "excepted" and "reserved" areas. "Excepted" subjects will remain with the UK unless the *Northern Ireland Act 1998* is amended. "Reserved" subjects could be transferred by Order at a later date if there is cross-community consent. This triple division of areas is unique to Northern Ireland devolution. Funding for the devolved institutions is mainly provided by a block grant calculated under the Barnett formula.

The West Lothian Question

The West Lothian Question has been regarded by many since the 1970s as a crucial consideration in any proposed devolution in the UK, and has been at the forefront of the current debate between the Government and Opposition parties. In its present form the Question can be constructed as whether 'Scottish' MPs should be entitled to sit and vote at Westminster on 'English' matters, while 'English' MPs are not be able to participate on equivalent matters devolved to a 'Scottish' Parliament. However, the Question, in the wider sense of symbolising the territorial asymmetry of devolution also encompasses related issues, such as the much-discussed level of representation of devolved areas at Westminster, Scottish MPs being ministers in 'English' departments and the practical and legal relationships between one or more devolved legislatures or assemblies and Westminster.

The 'author' of the Question is generally recognised as Tam Dalyell (Member for West Lothian in the 1970s), but the question was first posed in the nineteenth century as part of the controversy over Home Rule for Ireland.14 The West Lothian Question's importance rests, in part, on the perception that it is actually or virtually 'insoluble'.

Opponents of devolution use it as a political trump card against any devolution scheme, and pro-devolutionists often feel obliged to find a satisfactory 'answer' to it, such as a form of English regional devolution. However some commentators, such as Ferdinand Mount, have argued that the Question is neither insoluble nor a real problem, as it simply reflects the asymmetry common to British constitutional arrangements.15 Others have argued that the only way ahead is to have an English Parliament.

Difference between Scotland and Wales

A major difference between Scotland and Wales was that there was no parallel to the Scottish Constitutional Convention. The Welsh Labour Party refused overtures from the Campaign for a Welsh Assembly and in 1992 the Welsh Labour Executive established its own policy commission to consult on the proposed powers of an Assembly. In May 1996 *Preparing for a New Wales* was approved by the Conference. The White Paper, *A Voice for Wales*, was published on 22 July 1997, setting out the basis of the Welsh devolution settlement.[123]

---

[123] National Assembly for Wales Press Release (W001041-Ass), "Rhodri Morgan Announces New
'Partnership' Cabinet", 16 Oct 2000

Chapter 10 - The European Convention on Human Rights

Essay question 1

Should the UK have a Bill of Rights? Discuss.

Answer

Introduction

This essay will explain the workings of the Human Rights Act 1998 (HRA) and at the same time assess the impact it has had on our constitution and the courts. I will do this by first discussing the old English landscape in relation to the protection of human rights. Secondly this paper will explore the system of protection introduced by the European Court of Human Rights ("ECHR") and the impact it on the UK as a signatory to the Convention. Thirdly how the ECHR has incorporated human rights in the UK, and what alternative methods could have been utilised. Lastly this essay will address the impact which the HRA had on our constitution, in particular sections 3 and 4.

Traditional approach of the English Courts

Although the UK was the first country to approve the ECHR before the enactment of the HRA it was not willing to give the Convention any domestic support. Importance was not on human rights but upon civil liberties and negative freedom; where every citizen was permitted to do as they pleased as long as it was not restricted by an act. Thus there was no statement of fundamental rights, Dicey believed that protection was guaranteed in the common law, and this was sufficient. However Dicey's approach has limitation; in trying to maintain public order the law subsequently curtailed the exercise of certain freedoms, as there was nothing from preventing it doing so. This is evident in the case or **Malone v Metropolitan Police Commissioner [1979]** Ch 344 where **Megarry** held the police's action of telephone tapping was not unlawful as it was not specifically prohibited by law. The court in **R v Home Secretary, ex parte Brind [1991]** 1 AC 696 held the

Convention was not part of domestic law and the courts had no power in enforcing Convention rights. If civilians wished to rely upon their Convention rights the only option was to take their case to the European Courts of Human Rights (Strasbourg), but only after exhausting all other domestic remedies. The precarious and disorderly state of civil liberties in the UK before the HRA meant public authorities could disregard the Convention and the courts had no choice but to apply provisions even if they were in breach of the Convention. There was ample opportunity for citizens to assert their rights.

The Human Rights Act 1998

The incorporation of the ECHR became a fundamental policy of the Labour party in 1997 and following their success in the election the HRA was enacted in 1998. The HRA ensured a minimum guarantee of freedom to the citizens of the UK. It did not introduce any new rights but allowed the Convention rights to be enforced in the UK. Section 3 declares that the courts have an "obligation" to interpret in accordance with the Convention "so far as possible". Where an act is incompatible with the Convention, where there is no way of interpreting it in accordance with the Convention, the courts cannot apply a remedy other than a Declaration of Incompatibility (s.4 HRA). This does not have any effect upon the incompatible legislation, but just means it is passed onto Parliament to decide any further remedial action. Section 6 entails public authorities are bound by the Convention, they must act in accordance to it. There are two categories of 'public authorities', functional and core. Functional public authorities are only bound by the Convention on their public matters.

Alternative methods of incorporation of the ECHR into the UK have been explored by critics, in particular Kinley who suggested two joint committees, consisting of both Houses of Parliament examining bills to ensure they comply with the Convention. Another alternative would be a Human Rights Commissioner, to scrutinise legislation and investigate areas of concern.

Impact of the Human Rights Act

So should the HRA be in a written doctrine in order to firmly secure the protection of human rights? Governments have been hesitant to compile a written constitution as it would significantly restrict their policy making, as well as entailing a far larger judicial role giving them the ability to strike down legislation. The Conservative Government proposed to repeal the HRA and replace it with an entrenched 'British Bill of Rights', however due to the outcome of a coalition government this ceased to materialise.

Despite the HRA not being entrenched, thus not even having the power to immediately override inconsistent pre-existing acts it has still had a substantial effect on the UK's constitution. There is little doubt that the HRA achieved constitutional status immediately on its enactment and subsequently there has been a significant redistribution of powers within the constitution. Section 4 of the HRA entails that Parliament will carry out the will of the courts, rather than the orthodox relationship between Parliament and the judiciary.

There is also confusion as to whether the HRA is horizontally effective, can it be utilised from individual to individual. Wade argues Parliament's intentions are clear, that the HRA was to be horizontally effective. However, Richard Buxton and Lord Irvine disagree, arguing the HRA is purely vertically effective. The debate over this uncertainty continues.

Judiciary

Despite the judiciary not having the power to strike down breaching legislation the HRA has had a massive impact on the judiciary's interpretive role. They no longer have to find ambiguity in order to take account of the Convention rights when interpreting legislation. The scope of interpretation has been significantly widened. In **R v A (Complainant's Sexual History) (No 2) [2001]** 2 WLR 1546 a statute did not permit evidence to be used which would encroach on privacy, however this was argued a breach of the ECHR's right to a fair trial. Lord Steyn used s.3 to interpret the act in accordance with the Convention, by adding words to the relevant legislation. Whereas Lord Hope was of the opinion Lord Steyn had ignored Parliaments intentions and overstepped the boundaries of interpretation. The use of s.3 in this manner is also seen in the case of **Ghaidan v Godin-Mendoza**

[2004] UKHL 30where the Court of Appeal gave the Rent Act a modified meaning in order to make it compliant with the Convention. By the courts adding words and modifying legislation through the use of s.3 are they effectively legislating rather than interpreting? The extent of the power of s.3 has been debated; Klug and Starmer describe s.3 as a "radical tool" whereas Campbell plays down its power arguing s.3 controls a power which could undermine parliamentary sovereignty.

The Judiciary seem to have more power through s.3 than traditionally. However, when a statute is undeniably incompatible with the Convention, s.4 states a declaration of incompatibility can be made, which is then passed onto Parliament who makes the ultimate remedial decision. But it is the courts who decide between the uses of s.3 or s.4, using s.3 gives them the wide power of interpretation whereas s.4 gives the upper hand back to Parliament.

Conclusion

Since the enactment of the HRA, UK civilians have enjoyed a more accessible route to protect their Convention rights, one which is easier and far less expensive. However, citizens can still not be certain of the protection of their rights, as the courts have had an inconsistent approach to their interpretations of legislation; some judges cautious and others active.

Fundamentally the HRA has broadened the scope of the courts power, which enables them to actively protect the right to liberty; i.e. declaring the Anti-terrorism, Crime and Security Act 2001 incompatible. However the HRA limits this new found interpretative power, as the ultimate remedial power still remains with Parliament.

Chapter 11 - The Human Rights Act 1998

Essay Question 1

"The Human Rights Act has failed. What is needed is a Bill of Rights in the fullest sense of that term". Discuss

Answer

Introduction

If the Human Rights Act [1998] has failed, then it would appear the very source of its purpose has been wasted. Debates among constitutional lawyers over the incorporation of enforceable civil liberties have been rife ever since the formation of a new Labour Government in 1997. The UK's pre-Human Rights Act (HRA) era consisted of only citizens with extensive resources being able to enforce their human rights and even these select few could not do so in the UK. The European Court of Human Rights (ECtHR), situated in Strasbourg, was the primary source of enforcement of such rights and its power lay in the European Convention on Human Rights (ECHR) [1950]. The HRA has been legally notified as a domestic implementation of the principle criteria within the ECHR and it is mooted by many to hold much constitutional significance. Its influence has embodied what many believe to be the intention underlying an entrenched system in the UK for the protection of human rights.

Fenwick, H. argues that a Bill of Rights on the other hand, offers protection from State interference and is in effect, entrusted to the judiciary, on the basis that a government cannot be expected to keep a satisfactory check on itself[124]. The arguments surrounding the implementation of a written constitution in the UK and the benefits of such have been supported by many; even in recent comments from the Conservative leader Mr. Cameron, we see future intentions for the creation of a 'British Bill of Rights'. However, what it is meant in '*the fullest sense of that term*' will need to be considered against the integration of the HRA and it

---

[124] Fenwick, H, *Civil Liberties and Human Rights* (4th Ed., Routledge-Cavendish, 2007)

must be established whether or not the Act itself has come close enough or too far away from becoming in essence, a Bill of Rights.

The necessity of the Human Rights Act and the limitations of relying solely on the ECHR

It appears one very important reason behind the adoption of the HRA in the UK was due to the general, non-binding use of the Convention as a domestic tool. Especially the Thatcher Government, by introducing very little legislation protective of civil liberties, gave little aim or commitment to their enforceability; without a strict ruling from the ECtHR forcing them to do so. Was the HRA to make up for this? What are certainly true were the constitutional weaknesses in the government in holding to account and scrutinizing the actions of Ministers. The lack of a Freedom of Information Act gave the government power to present a selective picture of events. The HRA in effect, was able to preserve this Parliamentary supremacy but also give a check on standards of legislation being passed through government, ensuring Bills for example are accompanied by a statement of compatibility with the Convention[125]. When the Convention was the single source of such protection this accountability on Parliament was not required, therefore allowing Ministers to deviate from such responsibility. However, by merely declaring a Bill compatible, the House of Lords' attitude towards fundamental protection of human rights may be misplaced, as actual concerns over the effect of such protection could be allayed.

The case of *R v Secretary of State for the Home Department, ex parte Brind*[126] demonstrates ideally the role of the ECHR in UK law prior to the HRA. In situations where no domestic law states that compliance with an international instrument is necessary; members of the executive, e.g. the Home Secretary in this case, can simply dismiss such an external force completely. The law therefore surrounding the HRA can be justified as an entrenched check on the executive limiting such behaviour. How can this not

---

[125] HRA [1998], s. 19
[126] *R v Secretary of State for the Home Department, ex parte Brind* [1991] 1 All ER 720 (HL)

be done through a Bill of Rights? Taking the US Bill of Rights as an example, it can be seen as giving too much power to non-elected judges, because although judges can apply the HRA or a Bill of Rights through common law, their powers of interpretation are still subject to the will of Parliament. Parliamentary supremacy is an entrenched principle in UK domestic law and follows the much respected 'Rule of law'. A Bill of Rights would put much pressure on such a discipline being so highly entrenched and even though the HRA allows the courts to declare legislation incompatible with Convention rights[127], this is rare and courts willingly accept the authority of Parliament. The Human Rights Act therefore has succeeded in preserving the UK's comprehensive system of government, in allowing discretion of the executive but balancing this with an obligation on their part to fulfil obligations under the Act.

Would a British Bill of Rights enhance the protection of human rights in the UK?

The influential constitutional writings of Dicey, AV have bought into current relevance the traditional view on such a question[128]. Effectively, a Bill of Rights in the UK would become a deep-rooted constitution of the land, much to the same effect as the US Bill of Rights or Canadian Charter of Human Rights. Diceyan tradition holds that the absence of a written constitution in the UK is not a weakness, but a source of strength[129], encompassing the fact that through the common law system the law is passed through judicial decisions and precedent, not through the loose, unclear wording of constitutional documents. Now that most of the Convention rights have been incorporated into domestic law[130], they can have legal effect within the UK. It can be argued that a Bill of Rights would have the same result; it would be legally binding and answered to by the executive and judges alike. It has also been argued that the reason why the ECHR has been absorbed

---

[127] HRA [1998] s. 4

[128] See, Dicey, AV, *Introduction to the study of the Law of the Constitution,* 10th Ed, 1987, Macmillan

[129] Fenwick, H, *Civil Liberties and Human Rights* (4th Ed, Routledge-Cavendish, 2007) p. 123

[130] Not Articles. 1 or 13 ECHR

into UK law is in response to the high number of cases being taken to the ECtHR against the UK[131]. But in this sense the HRA can be seen as a resolution, allowing judges to interpret cases before them relying on a flexible, cohesive document.

Parliament through its enactment also have entrusted much power in judges, with sections 3 and 4 giving them the ability to interpret Convention rights as they see fit (discussed further in section 1.4). Simply put, such protection and adaptability offered through the HRA just would not be as available under a Bill of Rights, not to mention the lengthy and cumbersome amendment procedure needed for a written constitution.

The independent law reform and human rights organisation of JUSTICE in 2007, released a consultation paper entitled 'A Bill of Rights for Britain?'[132] The paper comprehensively outlines several convincing arguments supporting the introduction of such a document in the UK. A criticism which can be made of the paper from the outset however, are the intentions of JUSTICE to reform the law, not as to replace the HRA but include a Bill of Rights to enhance the protection the current Act affords. This would appear sensible, but when one considers the extent of political and public consensus concerned, it appears in evidence of its enforcement that the HRA is more achievable. Indeed, one of the very purposes for the inclusion of such a Bill according to JUSTICE is to 'build public awareness of constitutional rights' protection and enhance its legitimacy through public consultation', offering no practical method of accomplishing this.

Strength however in the content of such a Bill of Rights and highlighted in the discussion paper, is the additional rights to those contained within the ECHR which can be offered, i.e. relating to equality, economic and social rights. But the question lingers still over the fact that such rights are already offered protection under domestic legislation, e.g. the Race Relations Act 1976. By announcing this, what these arguments for a Bill of Rights appear

---

[131] See Bonner, D, *Rights, Liberties and the protection of the Individual* (University of Leicester Lecture Series) LW 2061/2062
[132] JUSTICE Constitution Project, '*A Bill of Rights for Britain*' http://www.justice.org.uk accessed 3rd January, 2008

to be achieving, are reasons hardly related to the HRA or human rights at all, but rather a strong legal base upon which to build an entirely separated system of law.

The debate remains as to whether the HRA, by combining the Convention with UK law, has effectively become a substitute for a Bill of Rights. In such case, wouldn't claiming that the Human Rights Act has failed be predicting the failure of a Bill of Rights also? Of course all this presuming they are intended as one of the same thing. But what the HRA offers for the UK, in defending the honour of our unwritten constitution by employing domestic recourse to litigants, goes further in its application than a Bill of Rights and Convention combined due to its versatile nature. We see in cases such as ***R (Al Skeini and others) v Secretary of State for Defence***[133] that in the instance of public authorities, the HRA can be used when dealing with people abroad. Article 1 states that High Contracting Parties must guarantee rights to everyone within their jurisdiction. This case concerned the UK's jurisdiction over killings in Iraq by British soldiers and although it was argued that the HRA should not apply in Iraq, the House of Lords ruled that in certain circumstances it can and proper investigations into the deceased must be granted under section 2. This demonstrates the shear velocity of the HRA and how far the UK's highest court will go to abide by it, something a Bill of Rights may have difficulty achieving through stringent code and practice.

The impact of the Human Rights Act 1998

The HRA is not an entrenched legal document, but nevertheless holds that clear language is essential if it is to be amended. As mentioned this may be seen as a success due to the rigorous constitutional procedure required to amend a Bill of Rights. It is also defendable that the greater powers of interpretation given to judges would not be available under a Bill, as its overriding governance leaves little scope for adjustability, the need for which is certain in today's volatile society. Croft, J, highlights in his paper *'Whitehall and the Human Rights Act 1998'* that consideration within the executive makes the HRA a national

---

[133] *R (Al Skeini and others) v Secretary of State for Defence* [2007] UKHL 26; [2007] 3 All ER 685

measure of proof against which all legislation must now be passed[134]. This inevitably controls the controversial view that a Bill of Rights would offer a greater legal base upon which to ensure the protection of human rights. The government's responsibility under section 19, HRA, means they are constantly required to have fundamental human rights at the heart of every Bill considered, offering a level of protection akin to an entrenched legal doctrine.

On the scrutiny of the actions of Parliament itself in relation to the application and successes of the HRA, the role of the Joint Houses of Commons/House of Lords Select Committee on Human Rights (JHRC) is relevant. Their reports on the examination of legislation demonstrate that apart from the responsibilities given to Parliament under the HRA itself, a secondary body is in place to ensure the legitimacy given to primary legislation with regard to compatibility. Their role even covers the Government's response to court judgements, helping to find any breach of human rights[135]. It becomes evident therefore that the protection the Human Rights Act offers does extend beyond its wording, but whether or not this as a result becomes a necessary manoeuvre is a concern, especially considering comments made by Andrew Dismore MP, the Chair of the JHRC. He concerts that the HRA is portrayed by the media as 'misunderstanding' but reserves the view that it is 'worth saving...if it can be made relevant'. His view is interesting when considering what the HRA offers and whether or not its application will now require a complete change in legal and social attitudes if it is to be effective. Perhaps a Bill would not require this; because of the HRA's openness to interpretation and supportive, more easily changeable values it can be said that society may feel too forced to embrace something more entrenched and not as easily amendable. Surely the challenge of helping ordinary people understand what rights they now have under the HRA would be better brought if the UK can feel warmth toward the accessible protection it offers.

---

[134] Croft, J, *'Whitehall and the Human Rights Act 1998'* [2001] European Human Rights Law Review 392
[135] See JHRC 16th Report (2006-07), *Monitoring the Government's Response to Court Judgements Finding Breaches of Human Rights,* HL 128/ HC 728

The role(s) of the courts is an influential factor in determining the successes, or failures of the Act in question also, in the reiteration of their interpretive role through the HRA. Previous case-law covered by the ECHR also, because of its authority over those signatory to it, must still be taken account of, whether by judgement, decision or advisory opinion of the ECtHR[136], in so far as it is relevant to the case as hand. This has been highlighted by Lord Irvine LC, as a way of permitting UK courts to depart from existing Strasbourg decisions where appropriate, but such a decision may lead back to Strasbourg[137] so this section of the Act must be used when absolutely necessary. Having the ECtHR as a final port of call can be seen as a weakness or strength depending on how the HRA is invoked. On one hand, they are available to give assistance and apply the Convention where the interpretation of the HRA falls short but on the other, this may display a lack of domestic coherence with the HRA and its provisions. A Bill of Rights used in such context may provide a sound framework by which to use its content in a manner best suited to the cause, but not every solution can be predicted. Therefore a Bill of Rights may cause difficulties where its terms may be too general to reach good judgement on the facts, but whether or not the interpretive duties under the Bill would give judges the same powers of interpretation as under the HRA is not clear.

Arguably the most influential provision contained within the HRA is section 3, which according to subsection (1), gives the courts a discretionary power to interpret all legislation in accordance with Convention rights 'so far as it is possible to do so'. With this, courts can interpret primary and subordinate legislation broadly so it is caught by this requirement. A key authority surrounding the use of section 3 is the case of *Ghaidan v Godin-Mendoza (FC)*[138], where the provisions' effects can be seen as giving power to courts to decide away from Parliaments intentions, which attaches many dangers to the legislator-interpreter relationship. The case concerned the question of whether Godin could succeed to the tenancy of a deceased homosexual partner. Was homosexuality

---

[136] HRA [1998] s. 2(1), (a)
[137] Lord Irvine LC, 583 HL Hansard, 514 (18th November 1997)
[138] *Ghaidan v Godin-Mendoza (FC)* [2004] UKHL 30; [2004] 3 All ER 411

compatible with existing law giving tenancy to the *spouse* of the deceased, meant only for heterosexual couples? The House of Lords held that reading the provision in this way was not compatible with Article 8 of the Convention protecting Godin's right to private life. The courts therefore read the statute to mean living with a spouse *as if* a husband or wife. We see then that although judges should be wary of *'judicial vandalism'*, they still wish to use section 3 in a beneficial light, consistently keeping the substance of the original provision at bay but tweaking so as to create an enforcement of civil liberties in conjunction with the rights of the Convention. What may be seen by Parliament as challenging the purpose of the initial legislation, can be seen as the courts showing respect for the intentions of the HRA through the use of such a power. It is questionable whether this inter-relationship would be as effective under an established, more tightly controlled system of enforcement under a Bill of Rights.

Where the use of section 3 in the *Godin* case may be seen as a necessary departure from original legislation passed by the government, the case of **R v A**[139] brings into understanding a further extreme of its potential. It is a criminal case concerning a rape shield provision affecting the defendant who was facing a charge of rape. It stipulated a limited duty on the defence when cross-examining witnesses and also placed limits on the prosecution when questioning victims. Section 3 was invoked by the courts who allowed further questions if the trial judge felt it necessary to secure a fair trial. Where judges may here be seen as going as far as legislating law, the true source of section 3 must not be forgotten. Cases such as **Bellinger v Bellinger**[140]demonstrate that the courts do only feel they are doing the duty required of them and that section 3 cannot be bent and shaped to accommodate all cases they face. In this sense, to submit the failure of the HRA would admit to ignoring what has become a logical step in maintaining a system of human rights protection which allows for failure, because without trial and error it would be near impossible to offer standardised security to all those who seek it. If the trial judge has no say under the stringent practise and application of a Bill of Rights, then situations will inevitably arise where faith in

---

[139] *R v A* [2001] All ER 1
[140] *Bellinger v Bellinger* [2003] UKHL 21; [2003] 2 All ER 593

the judgment of the courts will be lost to a paralysed mode of order, relieving the need for principles or safety accumulated through common law technique.

In fact, looking to the purpose of primary legislation passed by Parliament – the purposive interpretative approach – has been seen as an even more popular method used by judges since the HRA has been in force, as reiterated by J. Van Zyl Smit, who points out a heightened degree on purposive legislation[141], especially after the decision reached in the *Godin-Mendoza* case. What becomes apparent in reality is the reluctance of the courts to order against existing legislation; but what is now possible under section 4 of the HRA has caused much friction, where the courts may declare legislation incompatible with a Convention right. However, as mentioned this power has been rarely used and Parliament maintains that the courts still and will continue to have no power to invalidate a statute[142]. The courts reserve discretion however over the use of this power, which seems sensible considering its use, as under subsection (2) they may make the declaration only '[i]f the court is satisfied'. Although to say that this feature of the HRA is a success in keeping a check on the law created by Parliament would be an over statement of its real capacity, as evident in its sub provisions and through case-law such as *Bellinger*; its remedial actions can be seen as weak due to the courts constant deference to Parliament on situations they feel the executive are more equipped to handle.

Surely, the fact that section 19 is in place to ensure all legislation passed is compatible with Convention rights in the first place means little need for section 4 to be consequently enforced. But it is a mode of law, an ability to place political and legal pressure on the Government to conform to modern standards of protection. In this light it can most certainly be described as a defining feature of the HRA and this success of obligation alone demonstrates willingness by our highest authority to place an exceptional amount of trust in the courts and their abilities to apply and create

---

[141] Van, J, Zyl Smit *'The New Purposive Interpretation of Statutes: HRA section 3 after the Ghaidan v Godin-Mendoza'* (2007) 70 Modern Law Review 294
[142] HRA [1998] s. 4, (6)

the legal doctrines of the land. As pointed out by Leigh and Lustgarten however, section 4 affords the litigant no real remedy[143], which may be a fundamental feature of a Bill of Rights in full, where an applicant would be required through the ECHR to exhaust all domestic remedies before proceeding to Strasbourg. If however, section 4 of the HRA is invoked, an applicant may not be required to pursue their claim in domestic courts if the only remedy available is through a declaration of incompatibility. This is concerning for Parliament where it is for them to decide whether or not to amend legislation, but at-least through the HRA this option *is* available to them, albeit in a far more controlled setting.

Conclusion

One key element of the Human Rights Act in this writer's opinion is its aptitude and constant focus on not entrenched law, but entrenched systems and mechanisms surrounding the law's application. Parliament passes the law and courts apply the law to the best of their abilities to a given and regularly unpredictable factual scenario. The successes of the HRA as discussed keep in place the doctrines of important legal status, such as those governing the working relationship between Parliament and the courts. A Bill of Rights *'in the fullest sense of that term'* is not needed, as although its binding solidarity would create set law upon which to construct a decision, it would never match up to those components under the HRA, such as the powers granted under sections 3 and 4. These allow fundamental human rights to be protected under a practise determined by the very nature of its intentions rather than from an insoluble form of law inadaptable to the changing morals of the land. The HRA is in essence, a success *in the fullest sense of that term* in the amendable, practical security it affords.

---

[143] Leigh and Lustgarten, *'Making Rights Real: The Courts, Remedies and the Human Rights Act'* (1999) 58 Cambridge Law Journal 509

Chapter 12 – Articles 2, 3, 5 & 6 ECHR

Problem Question 1

The recent conflicts in the Middle East have led to a rise in people coming to the UK to claim refugee status. The Home Office claims that this increases the risk that people intent on carrying out acts of terrorism will come to the UK. In order to address this risk, the Home Office develops an elaborate scheme for "Muslim refugees", once they arrive in the UK, to be detained and transported to No Way Island, just off the coast of Kent, UK. Their detention is indefinite. The Home Office has also contracted a private company, Refugee Solutions, to manage and run the detention facility on No Way Island.

Parliament has passed legislation, the Ban on Muslim Refugees Act 2017, to facilitate the scheme. The UK also issues a Derogation Order under Article 15 of the European Convention on Human Rights to exempt the operation of Articles 5 and 14 of the Convention.

Leila, a woman detained on No Way Island, would like to challenge the policy of indefinite detention and the operation of the Ban on Muslim Refugees Act 2017. She would like to do this on her own behalf as well as on behalf of all other detainees.

a) Advise Leila.

b) How would you advise the Government in meeting the challenge by Leila?

c) How would you determine the matter if you were the judge in the case?

Answer all components of this question.

* Note: The Ban on Muslim Refugees Act 2017, is hypothetical and not actual legislation. Your answer need NOT refer to immigration law. It is your knowledge of the operation of

the Human Rights Act 1998, and judicial review that is being assessed

Answer

Introduction

This is an advice in relation to the scheme for "Muslim refugees", that are detained and transported to No Way Island, just off the coast of Kent, UK. This advice will a) Advise Leila; b) advise the Government in meeting the challenge by Leila; and c) determine the matter as if the judge in the case?

a) Advice to Leila

Leila, a woman detained on No Way Island, would like to challenge the policy of indefinite detention and the operation of the Ban on Muslim Refugees Act 2017. Leila can bring an action under Article 5 of the HRA and ECHR and Article 14 of the same.

Preliminary issues

1. The first thing to establish Leila is (the appellant) a victim? (s 7 HRA; Art 34 ECHR) (Klass v Germany - 'applicants must show that they are directly affected by state action in order to be a victim'). The answer is yes she is the victim.

2. Is the body interfering with the right a 'public authority – s6(1)? Is it core and liable for all that is done, or functional/ hybrid (Aston Cantlow – 'the concept of public authorities – both core and functional'). Yes the Home Office is a 'core' public authority.

3. Is the claim within the one year time limit (s 7(5)(a)) or in a period that the tribunal considers equitable (s 7 (5)(b))? - yes the claim is within the prescribed time.

4. 4) Was the act complained of within the UK jurisdiction (Al-Skeini and Others v Secretary Of State For Defence – Art 1 ECHR) - Yes, the act is within the UK jurisdiction.

Article 5

The next step is to determine if there has been an infringement of article 5 right. The following determinations need to be made.

- **Was the arrest a deprivation of liberty justified by one of the acceptable limitations in the Article?**
- **Was the interference prescribed by law?**
- **What can be done about any violation under the HRA?**

Guarantees against arbitrary detention are provided by the ECHR, art 5. A detention may be lawful where someone is imprisoned. ECHR, art 5 is engaged where a person has been deprived of their liberty. Strasbourg has noted that this may take numerous forms. Determining whether there has been a deprivation of liberty so as to engage the ECHR, art 5 is a question of degree or intensity of the restriction placed upon freedom of movement, and the general extent to which the state regulates control over the individual. Article 5 of the ECHR is a complicated article, structurally. Article 5(1) of the ECHR firstly provides for the substantive right of liberty itself. It then goes on to say that no one can be deprived of their liberty unless this is done 'in accordance with a procedure prescribed by law'.

It has to be determined if the detention of Leila was prescribed by law. In accordance/ prescribed by law – *Sunday Times v UK* 1979- TEST

1)   Is there a legal basis for the interference with a right?

These are contained under the six specific circumstances outlined in sub-paragraphs (a)–(f). These sub-paragraphs define a variety of situations in which a person may be legitimately deprived of their liberty by the state. The relevant section is article 5(1)(f) which states no one shall be deprived of their liberty except where:

"the lawful arrest or detention of a person to prevent his effecting an unauthorised entry into the country or of a person against whom action is being taken with a view to deportation or extradition."

The exception to the right seems to apply here. Over the fear of terrorism and the rising number people coming to the UK to claim refugee status the Home Office introduced an elaborate scheme for "Muslim refugees", once they arrive in the UK, to be detained and transported to No Way Island. Their detention is indefinite.

2)   Is the relevant law sufficiently accessible to the affected individual and sufficiently precise?

Is the relevant law sufficiently accessible to the affected individual and sufficiently precise? - The Ban on Muslim Refugees Act 2017 is an act of Parliament thus is sufficiently accessible. Arguably, the Act is not precisely clear because it is not clear how it can be determined whether someone's poses the risk of terrorism. It is just a blanket ban on persons from the Middle East have led to a rise in people coming to the UK to claim refugee status.

3)   If the above two factors are satisfied, has the interference nevertheless have been carried out in an arbitrary way (in bad faith or disproportionally)?

Yes, it appears to be disproportionate because the Act clearly states the detention is indefinite, without being promptly brought before a judge, is arguably this is disproportionate. In *R (on the application of Saadi) v Secretary of State for the Home Department* [2002] UKHL 41, the House of Lords held that detention of asylum seekers for the purpose of enabling the authorities to decide whether to authorise entry into the UK was allowed by the ECHR, art 5(1)(f), as long as they were detained in reasonable conditions and not for excessive periods.

Even if a person has been lawfully arrested and detained within the terms of the ECHR, art 5, it is also important to ask: (c) Has there been an interference by the state with one or more of the due process rights protected in paragraphs 2–4 of the ECHR, art 5?

Article 5(4) of the ECHR states that a person who is arrested and detained 'shall be entitled' ('speedily') to challenge in court the lawfulness of the action taken against them. In *Hirst v UK* (2001) ECHR 477, the ECtHR held that delays of 21 months and 2 years between reviews of the applicant's continued detention amounted to a breach of the ECHR, art 5(4). In *T and V v UK* (2000) 30 EHRR 121, the ECtHR held that the ECHR, art 5(4) had been violated because there had been no judicial control of the applicants' detention. The Home Secretary, rather than a court, had decided on the length of the tariff to be served and there had been no form of review.

Articles 14

The emergency of the situation might be questioned in this case, as Leila as a refugee was suspected of terrorism and detained under the Ban on Muslim Refugees Act 2017. It needs to be taken into account the information and the evidence that the Home Office has in relation to this issue, and considered if this information is sufficient enough to justify the damages that Leila suffered. Refuges from non-Middle East countries are not subject to this treatment. Therefore, different treatment and different procedure in relation detention is followed by the Home Office and it might be argued that this problem applies only to Muslim refugees. In *A and Others* derogation was entered in respect of Art 5(1), however the HL held that the power to detain foreign nationals in circumstances where British nationals could not be detained was discriminatory and therefore in breach of Art 14. To sum up, the given case is more likely to succeed if it reaches the European Court of Human Rights, who may find that the UK law is incompatible with the convention, taking into account the idea in *A and Others* that the idea of the rule of law is the need properly to constrain and control executive action.

Use of Human Right Act

If a statutory provision is found to be incompatible with a Convention right, the court is likely to interpret the offending provision consistently with the relevant Convention right (using s3). Under section 3 HRA - Can the court use this section to interpret the Ban on Muslim Refugees Act 2017 in such a way as to make it compatible with the ECHR? In *R v A*, Lord Steyn advocated a wide approach to interpretation of statutes using s.3. Lord Hope on the other hand took a narrower approach (see also *Bellinger v Bellinger* and *Re S*)'. If the court cannot interpret the Ban on Muslim Refugees Act 2017 to be compatible with the Leila's ECHR rights, it may make a declaration of incompatibility under s. 4 If the Home Office have acted unlawfully s.6 (1) HRA, Leila would be entitled to remedy under s8 of the HRA.

Judicial review

The Act which has detained Leila is a public law legislative Act which Parliament has passed. The aim has been to facilitate the scheme devised by the Home office. The blanket ban the Act places on all Muslim refugees is reviewable by the High court. A claim for Judicial review ("JR") can be brought under s31 of the Supreme Court Act 1981. The procedure is found in the Civil Procedure Rules, part 54.

The procedure for making an application for JR has two stages: (1) An application for permission (previously called 'leave') must be made to the Administrative Court. Here an applicant will only be granted permission if they have standing ('sufficient interest') in the matter before them and the application is made within time (3 months).[144] (2) Main Hearing. Applicants must have grounds to challenge the decision. Where an individual is directly affected by a decision, that individual will clearly have sufficient interest; *R v Secretary of State for Home Department ex p Venables* [1998] AC 407 (HL). Leila will have standing in an action for herself but not for all other detainees. However if the Act is held to be unlawful it will bring about the necessary change in the law.

If we take into account *A and others v The Secretary of State for the Home Department*, 2004, it might be argued that if the issue concerns National Security, and the Home Secretary reasonably believes that that person is to be of hostile association, arrest without warrant could be conducted only if certain legal

---

[144] *R v Dairy Produce Quota Tribunal ex p Carswell [1990] 2 C 438 (HL)*

requirements are covered. The ministers and the civil servants are subject to the court jurisdiction. Thus, more information about the given (fictitious) The Ban on Muslim Refugees Act 2017 Act is required. The three grounds for a judicial review action are illegality, irrationality and procedural impropriety. The Act is likely to be defended on the grounds of national security as they did in *GCHQ*. The courts are more reluctant to review decisions relating to social and economic policy, i.e. they operate a high degree of deference (and therefore lower intensity of review) to the decision-maker in such circumstances.

b) Advice to Government in meeting the challenge by Leila

The UK also issues a Derogation Order under Article 15 of the European Convention on Human Rights to exempt the operation of Articles 5 and 14 of the Convention. Article 5 of the ECHR is a limited right, which can be subject to derogation in emergency situations. Indeed, the UK did lodge a derogation to the ECHR, art 5 with respect to individuals detained on suspicion of involvement in terrorist activities (the 'Belmarsh detainees'), when it made the Human Rights Act 1998 (Designated Derogation) Order 2001 (SI 2001/3644)). That derogation was withdrawn in 2005. The detention under The Ban on Muslim Refugees Act 2017 will then be lawful because it was incompatible with article 5(1) of the European Convention on Human Rights Act. Moreover, in *A and Others v The Home Secretary for the Home Department*, the UK had to act in a manner that was incompatible with article 5 and 14 of the Convention, this the UK had to derogate from the ECHR under Article 15 of the convention, and Parliament passed the Anti-Terrorism, Crime and Security Act 2001 which allowed detention of non-nationals suspected of terrorism. Looking at the facts, it needs to be considered whether the act in Leila v UK is worthy of the derogation.

c) Determine the matter as the judge in the case

The Ban on Muslim Refugees Act 2017 will be reviewable even though the court does not in theory permitted to overrule Acts of Parliament. Thus, in *R v Secretary of State for the Home*

Department ex p Javed [2001] EWCA 789, the Court of Appeal held that the Minister had acted irrationally when he made a Statutory Instrument, which designated Pakistan as a country in which 'in general there is no risk of persecution'; adding it to a so-called 'white list'. This designation had the effect of denying all asylum-seekers from that country a right of appeal against refusal of asylum. Given the abundance of evidence that persecution was very widespread in Pakistan at the time, the Court held that the decision to designate Pakistan was incomprehensible and, therefore, irrational.

The issue of the breach of human rights and the review of the operation of the Ban on Muslim Refugees Act 2017, is something that will be reviewed by the judge in the same application. This is likely to be review where the human right issue is stated to arise. In *GCHQ*, Lord Diplock acknowledged that in future there might be additions to the three heads of review, which he identified. One of these grounds was proportionality. The doctrine of proportionality requires that the means employed by the decision-maker to achieve a legitimate aim must be no more than is reasonably necessary to achieve that aim. The status of proportionality as a ground of review in UK law was considered by the House of Lords in *R v Secretary of State for the Home Department ex p Brind* [1991]. The judge will find in favour of the Leila over the Ban on Muslim Refugees Act 2017, because the effect of the Act are too far reaching with no procedural safeguard. This blanket ban will cause the unnecessary usurping of rights of many innocent individuals. The Act is disproportionate in the aim it is trying to peruse. More proportionate response would be the use of control order.

In response to the decision in *A and Others*, provision was made in the Prevention of Terrorism Act 2005 for the making of control orders. These orders were designed to control the movements and activities of certain individuals for the purpose of providing protection against terrorist activity. Control orders can contain conditions such as bans on all forms of communication including mobile phone and internet use, travel and movement restrictions, curfews, restrictions on those with whom a person can associate, and electronic tagging. Unlike the detention regime successfully challenged in A and Others, control orders were designed to be non-discriminatory and could apply to foreigners or British citizens. Under the Prevention of Terrorism Act 2005, provision was made for the Home Secretary to apply to the High Court to make a derogating control order. Such an order would allow the conditions, which constitute the substance of the control order, to go beyond what would be allowed under the ECHR, art 5. A formal derogation from the requirements of the ECHR, art 5 would then have to be made by the Home Secretary before a derogating control order could be issued. These provisions have never been utilised.

Chapter 13 - The right to family life - Article 8 ECHR

Essay Question 1

"We have reached a point at which it can be said with confidence that the law recognises and will appropriately protect a right of personal privacy." Sedley LJ in Douglas v Hello! Ltd. (No.1) [2001] 2 WLR 992.

"I do not understand Sedley LJ to have been advocating the creation of a high-level principle of invasion of privacy. His observations are in my opinion no more than a plea for the extension...of...breach of confidence...There [is] a great difference between identifying privacy as a value which underlies the existence of a rule of law (and may point the direction in which the law should develop) and privacy as a principle of law in itself." Lord Hoffman in Wainwright v Home Office [2003] 3 WLR 1137.

Consider whether it is time that the Supreme Court declared there to be a tort of invasion of privacy, or whether an individual's right to privacy is already adequately protected. Support your argument with relevant authority.

Answer

Before examining how it is regarded and analysed in a legal context, it is useful to ask what the definition of privacy is. That is, what does the concept mean to us on an everyday basis. The Oxford dictionary provides two definitions of 'privacy': (1) " *A state in which one is not observed or disturbed by other people*" and (2) *"The state of being free from public attention "*. When we consider each of these definitions carefully we can understand how, on an everyday basis, a life without any privacy would seem to be inconceivable. Maintaining the privacy of our inner lives allows space for psychological well-being and maturation, for creativity and for the development of intimate and trusting relationships with others. Some have argued that the reason Marilyn Monroe, one of the world's most famous actresses, committed suicide was because her life was entirely public and exposed. Indeed, this may be argued for many tragic cases of suicide among celebrities or public figures. Our relationship with, and concept of, privacy is changing.

Privacy is a hot topic today, both in the legal system and in society in general, because of the massive changes in the way we live over the past two decades. It is more and more difficult to be in a state where one is not observed or disturbed by others or where one is free from public attention, because of the widespread intrusion of, for example, mobile phones and smart phones, cameras, videos, CCTV surveillance, GPS, Google Earth and internet cookies (even if we are innocently browsing the internet at home alone, our movements are likely being tracked, monitored and stored). Arguably, one has to go on a technology-free retreat in the wilderness to be guaranteed this state. Interestingly, on the other hand, this increased exposure of our lives to public attention has blurred the lines between what we consider private and public. Many of us willingly share private and intimate information publicly through social media like Facebook, Twitter, Youtube and Blogs so much so that Facebook CEO, Mark Zuckerburg has said privacy is no longer the "*social norm*" and " *People have really gotten comfortable not only sharing more information and different kinds, but more openly and with more people*". It is true that our levels of comfort with living our lives more and more publicly have changed. In particular, the younger generation today cannot imagine a world without internet, smart phones, Facebook and Twitter while the older generation are struggling to adapt to life with these additions.

The idea of privacy as a legally protected right in fact originated in the US well over a century ago when an article entitled 'The Right to Privacy' was published in the influential Harvard Law Review by two attorneys, Samuel D Warren and Louis D Brandeis. The article achieved legendary status and led to the birth of the legal recognition of privacy in the US in the early part of the 20th century. Notably, and arguably far more relevant today than at the time it was published, the article referred to "*the intensity and complexity of life*" and argued that invasions of privacy subjected a person to "*mental pain and distress, far greater than could be inflicted by mere bodily injury*" and that people needed to be protected. Today, unlike in the UK, modern tort law in the US offers comprehensive protection in the form of four categories for invasion of privacy. They are: (a) intrusion upon the plaintiff's seclusion or solitude or private affairs; (b) public disclosure of embarrassing private facts about the plaintiff; (c) publicity which places the plaintiff in a false light in the public eye; and (d) appropriation, for the defendant's advantage, of the plaintiff's name or likeness.

Despite these developments in the US, privacy as a legally protected right was far slower to develop in the UK. It was finally recognised when the European Convention on Human Rights (ECHR) was implemented into UK law by way of the *Human Rights Act* 1998 (UK). Article 8 of the ECHR explicitly provides a right to respect for one's "private and family life, his home and his correspondence" subject to certain restrictions. This leads to the consideration, having regard to this significant development in 1998 in the UK, of whether an individual's right to privacy today is adequately protected by the law. In my view, there is adequate protection available today. A rapid evolution of the law of privacy in the UK has happened since 1998 with the Courts finding themselves obliged to give appropriate consideration and effect to Article 8 in the cases that come before them. A review of the significant case law is developed further below. However, it is worth first mentioning that there are numerous other laws which protect aspects of life in which invasions of privacy can occur. By way of example, privacy on your land and in your own home is protected through the cause of action of private nuisance; privacy of your personal space and bodily integrity is protected through the criminal action of battery and perhaps to a great extent by the Protection from Harassment Act 1997; the right to have your personal and professional reputation maintained is protected by the tort of defamation; and finally data protection legislation offers considerable protection for our private information and data when shared.

Most importantly, as referred to above, the Courts have been developing and expanding the law of privacy (without going as far as declaring a tort of invasion of privacy) through the equitable law of breach of confidence to encompass misuses of private information. It has recently been acknowledged by the Court in *Judith Vidal-Hall & ors v Google Inc* [2014] EWHC 13 that there is now an independent tort for misuse of private information.

It is worth examining a selection of the most important cases chronologically to consider how the issue has been discussed and dealt with:

Douglas v Hello! Ltd [2001] QB 967, involved the unauthorised and surreptitious taking, and selling to Hello! magazine, of wedding photographs of the celebrity wedding of Michael Douglas and Catherine Zeta-Jones by a freelance photographer. While the Court made the important acknowledgement in that case that *"We have reached a point at which it can be said with confidence that the law recognises and will appropriately protect a right of personal privacy"* ultimately it was held that the claim could be dealt with under the equitable law of breach of confidence.

Campbell v Mirror Group Newspapers Ltd [2004] UKHL 22, involved well-known celebrity model Naomi Campbell suing Mirror Group Newspapers for breach of confidence over published photographs of her leaving a Narcotics Anonymous meeting. In that case it was stated that the cause of action for breach of confidence *" has now firmly shaken off the limiting constraint of the need for an initial confidential relationship"* and that it should more appropriately be referred to as a cause of action for 'misuse of private information' since the law now imposes a *"duty of confidence"* whenever a person receives information he knows or ought to know is fairly and reasonably to be regarded as 'confidential' or, what is more appropriately termed 'private'.

Wainwright v Home Office [2004] 2 AC 406 involved a strip search of the plaintiffs who had gone to visit a relative in prison. The search had been conducted in accordance with the prison rules and was carried out in a manner which was calculated, in an objective sense, to humiliate and cause distress to the plaintiffs. Lord Hoffman emphatically confirmed that there was no common law tort of invasion of privacy and that the general opinion of the judiciary was that legislating in the area of privacy was a matter for Parliament rather than 'the broad brush of common law principle'.

ETK v News Group Newspapers Ltd [2011] EWCA Civ 439 involved an application for an injunction to stop the publishers of the News of the World Newspaper publishing, communicating or disclosing to any other person information relating to the identity of ETK or details of the sexual relationship between ETK and 'X', a person named a confidential schedule to the application. This case is useful as the Court summarised the steps which govern an application for an interim injunction to restrain publicity of private information. They are:

(a) First step: whether the applicant has a reasonable expectation of privacy so as to engage Article 8 of the ECHR. If this criteria is not present the application will automatically fail. A decision as to whether a reasonable expectation of privacy exists will take all of the circumstances into account and generally uses a test of whether a reasonable person of ordinary sensibilities, if placed in the same situation as the subject of the disclosure, would find the disclosure offensive. Protection may be lost if the information is already in the public domain;

(b) Second step: this step involves a balancing exercise with the right of freedom of expression in Article 10 of the ECHR. The decisive factor is the contribution which the information the subject of the disclosure makes to a debate of general interest.

In conclusion, an acknowledgement that the law of privacy in the UK is adequate today equally acknowledges the fact that the common law is constantly in a state of flux and evolution. As our society changes, and our concepts of privacy change, so to must the Courts be prepared to deal creatively with the cases of invasion of privacy that come before them as, I would argue, they have done to date by expanding upon breach of confidence law and developing the tort of misuse of private information. When one considers the definition of privacy one starts to appreciate the difficulties encountered by both the legislature and the judiciary, and their reluctance, in attempting to construct uniform laws, regulations and rules around that definition. As Chief Justice Gleeson noted in the Australian case of *ABC v Lenah Game Meats Pty Ltd* (2001) 208 CLR 199 " *the lack of precision of the concept of privacy is a reason for caution in declaring a new tort of the kind for which the respondent contends .*" Some have argued that privacy itself is beyond the scope of the law because it is a natural human right in the same way as freedom is. Furthermore, like freedom, privacy can mean different things to different people depending, for example, on their upbringing, age group, gender, culture, global location, education or faith. Accordingly, the extent to which privacy may be seen to be invaded or intruded upon will depend on the individual and his or her relationship with society. Finally, I would venture to say that Mark Zuckerburg of Facebook may in the near future be proved right. As technology and interconnectivity continue to explode and expand privacy may eventually no longer be considered a social norm.

Chapter 14 – Freedom of Expression – Article 10 ECHR

Essay Question 1

The protection of individuals from defamation and the protection of the presses freedom of expression should be balanced. Discuss.

Answer

This paper will make a case for the repealing various defamation laws in relation to journalists. This change will be advocated because it sits uneasily with Article 10 of the European Convention on Human Rights ("ECHR") (as implemented into English Law through the Hum Rights Act 1998). This paper will argue that this although not stature law but rather common law should be repealed to prevent journalists being subject to the view that their right to freedom of expression preserved within Article 10 of the ECHR is at risk every time they produce a piece of work, the contents of which may lead to a finding of libel by defamation.[145]

What is the right preserved in Article 10, one may ask? Article 10 states that *"(1) Everyone has the right to freedom of expression. This right shall include freedom to hold opinions and to receive and impart information and ideas without interference by public authority and regardless of frontiers"* At present journalists whether newspaper or on television or radio, are subject to the provisions of Section 166 of the Broadcasting Act 1990. This legislation provides that the publication of defamatory words, pictures, gestures and other statements amounts to libel.[146] Steele defines defamation with reference to Lord Atkin's judgement in *Sim v Stretch*[147] as "exposing the plaintiff to hatred, ridicule and contempt" and lowering the planitiff in the estimation of right-thinking members of society generally.[148]

---

[145] M, Jones, "Textbook on Torts" (Blackstone Press Limited, 2000) Page 495

[146] T, Weir, "A casebook on Tort" (London, Sweet & Maxwell, 2004) page 520

[147] [1936] 2 All ER 1237

[148] as J, Steel, "Tort Law: Text, Case and Materials" (Oxford University Press, 2007) page 761

Arguably journalists play a crucial part in society by holding particularly individuals in power[149] to account as argued by J G Flemming in his book.[150] If they continue to be restrained in doing so by anti-defamation legislation, this arguably limits the extent of the important job that they do. This papers issue with the current legislation on defamation and regarding section 2 of the Defamation Act 1952, is that there is no requirement to prove special damage to show that Defamation has occurred.

This papers interpretation of this is that a journalist would not have to necessarily cause damage to an individual's reputation, when they have spoken against them on television or radio, the possibility that the words that they have used would be enough to render them liable for an action in defamation. Arguably despite the attempts in cases such as *Lewis v. Daily Telegraph*[151] to introduce some common sense into whether journalists should be held liable for what amount to be truthful statements, earlier cases such as *Hough v London Express* [152]serve to show that as regards innuendo, the person knowing the relevant facts does not need to understand the article to contain defamatory material.[153]

Despite my central rationale being that the legislation regarding defamation should be repealed, there have been attempts in case law to provide some defence for journalists, and in relation to preserving journalists' freedom of expression.[154] The fair comment defence clarified by Lord Denning in *Slim v Daily Telegraph*[155] was of particular significance summed as *"the right of fair comment is one of the essential elements which go to make up our*

---

[149] F, Trindade, "Defamatory Statements and Political Discusssion" (2000) 116 LQR 185, K, Williams, "Defaming Politicians: The not so Common Law" (2003) 63 MLR 748

[150] J, Fleming, "The Law of Torts (9th Edition, NSW: Law Book Company, 1998) Page 648

[151] [1964] AC 234

[152] [1940] 2 KB 507

[153] J, Steele *op cit* page 766

[154] (see also in relation to confidential information, page 1004 L, Bently and B, Sherman, "Intellectual Property law" (Oxford University Press, 2009) page 1002

[155][1968] 2 QB 157

freedom of speech. We must ever retain this right intact. It must not be whittled down by legal refinements".[156]

Furthermore, LJ Scott in ***Lyon v Daily Telegraph*** [157]clarified that *"The reason why, once a pleas of fair comment is established, there is no libel is that it is in the public interest to have a free discussion of matters of public interest."* There was a similar finding in ***Cheng v Tse Wai Chun Paul*[158]** , and in ***Reynolds v Times Newspapers Limited*,**[159] by Lord Denning. Moreover, in by Lord Porter in ***London Artists v Littler*,**[160] in ***Kemsley v Foot*,**[161] in ***Rupert Lowe v Associated Newspapers*[162]**, in ***Telnikoff v Matusevitch*[163]** and in ***Branson v Bower*.**[164]

The fact that there has been so much case law on this is welcome, but also significant. The reason for the proliferation of case law is that the courts have sought to fill the gap in the law relating to defamation to describe and define fully, why arguably there is no specific reference to the human rights of journalist in the existing legislation to express their views freely in pursuance of Article 10 of the European Convention on Human Rights.[165] The reason for the lack of specific defamation legislation to support the human rights of journalists maybe that the legislators have come to the view that the imposition of Article 10 of the European Convention of Human Rights into UK law by section 3 of the Human Rights Act 1998, was sufficient to impose also the right to freedom of expression for journalists.

However arguably this paper submits this was insufficient as

---

[156] E, Barendt, "Libel and Freedom of Speech in English Law [1993] PL 449
[157] [1943] KB 746
[158] [2000] 4 HKC 1 at page 14
[159] [2001] 2 AC 127
[160] [1969] 2 QB 375
[161] [1952] AC 345
[162] [2006] EWHC 320
[163] [1992] 2 AC 343
[164] [2002] QB 737
[165] Richardson & Thomas, "Archbold 2003" (Thomson Sweet & Maxwell) page 1544.

although Article 10 protects journalists' right to freedom of speech, it also restricts this right in relation to defamation. Article 10(2) of the ECHR state that *"the exercise of these freedoms, since it carries with it duties and responsibilities may be subject to such formalities, conditions, restrictions or penalties as are prescribed by law and are necessary in a democratic society .... For the protection of the reputation or rights or others."* This reference to reputation is very important. This papers proposal for the repeal of the law relating to defamation as regards journalists is that all the work of journalists should be free of an action in defamation. Yes arguably this is a very radical proposal however, my view is that journalists should be trusted and expected to use their professional judgment in embarking on their work. No doubt with this trust comes a great deal of responsibility. One proposal to curb journalists and the statements they make could be more professional conduct of journalists, such as a code of practice. However in its absence, depending on the view or rationale in a court under the current system if a journalist is faced with defamation proceedings, journalists run the risk of being found guilty of defamation, when they are merely performing their important role in society.

Further particularly in relation to publication or broadcasting as regards criminal prosecution the European Court of Human Rights is driven to draw an interference as occurred in cases such as *Handyside v UK, X Ltd v UK*[166] *Lingens v Austria*[167], Muller *v Switzerland,*[168] *Jersild v Denmark,*[169] *Otto-Premiger-Institut v Austria,*[170] *Prager and Obershclick v Austria*[171] and the UK case of *Goodwin v UK*[172][173] that it contravenes the right to freedom of expression. This papers Argument is that if a criminal prosecution relation to defamation mounts a challenge to freedom of expression a civil claim against journalist should also be deemed to

---

[166] 28 DR 77,
[167] 8 EHRR 407
[168] 18 EHRR 276
[169] 19 EHRR 1
[170] 19 EHRR 34
[171] 21 EHRR
[172] 22 EHRR 123
[173] Archbold *op cit* pages 1544-1545

be in contravention of journalists' right to free speech.

However the justification for my central thesis that the defamation legislation needs to be repealed in relation to journalists is best summed up by Lord Diplock in the 1980 case of **Gleaves v Deakin**[174] in which he said that the "English offence of defamatory libel was *"difficult to reconcile"* with Article 10.[175] This arguably marks the clear problem with the existing legislation. One cannot promote the freedom of expression in relation to journalists if this freedom is not reserved within the existing legislation.

One cannot also ignore the defences introduced with the update to the 1952 Act contained with section 1 of the Defamation Act 1996, particularly as regards reducing liability for defamation where an individual could show that (a) they were not the author, editor, (b) tool reasonable care and (c) did not know that what he caused contributed to the publication of the defamatory statement. However still the legislation does not deal with the particular idiosyncrasies faced by journalists.

In concession journalists although not specifically referred have the benefit of absolute privilege if they pursuant to section 14 of the Defamation Act 1996 if they make a fair and accurate report of judicial proceedings. However the fact that their remains the doctrine of *"qualified privilege at common law"*[176] demonstrates that there is a gap in the existing legislation. Even as in **Reynold v Times Newspapers Lt**d[177] and I. Loveland in "Reynolds v Times Newspapers in the House of Lords"[178] however the House of Lords was keen to restrict the protection that Times Newspaper sought in limiting the protection in relation to political speech as not unqualified, but restricted to only certain publications to the world at large. Although arguably the ratio was useful in clarifying the law somewhat, the lack of specific legislation on the point means that in future cases there will be a level of inconsistency over the potential findings, such as occurred **in Al-Fagih v HH Saudi**

---

[174] [1980] AC 477 HL
[175] Archbold *op cit* page 1545
[176] J, Steele op cit page 783,
[177] [2001] 2 AC 127 I
[178] [2000] PL 351

Research and Marketing (UK) Ltd. [179]

In conclusion the law of defamation should be repealed so as to be reconstituted to include the provision that journalists should be given free rein to publish their material without fear of a potential action in defamation. The inconsistencies in the common law justify this course of action and there is space for a Defamation (Journalist exceptions) Act 2010.

---

[179] [2001] EWCA Civ 1634

Chapter 15 – Judicial review: Preliminaries and procedure

Question

"The procedural restrictions for judicial review (such as sufficient interest and timeliness) are necessary to strike the correct balance between governance according to law and protecting public bodies from unnecessary interference with their work". Discuss.

Answer

This is a paper to establish whether the current system governing the application of judicial review (JR) is, to the best of our knowledge, in an efficient and socially acceptable state of affairs. To analyse this we will discuss the following.

1. Public function and accountability
2. The procedural restrictions of Judicial review
3. Judicial review as a remedy
4. Limitations of Judicial review
5. Conclusion

Public function and accountability

Our current society is reliant upon public body's to govern all individuals within its jurisdiction. These functions can include things such as the prevention of crime and the granting of planning permissions. In the course of justice, it is when these decisions inflict a detriment to an individual that the system of JR may be considered and the public body made accountable.

A public body is defined by **Lloyd, LJ** in **R v Panel of Takeovers and Mergers ex p Datafin 1987** with the following statement: "If the source of power is a statute, or subordinate legislation under a statute, then clearly the body in question will be subject to judicial review...if the body is exercising a public law function, or if the exercise of its functions have public law consequences, then that may be sufficient to bring the body within the reach of judicial review". The term "public function" is largely ambiguous and has thus caused a large amount of uncertainty. It was, for example, decided that as per **R v Advertising Standards Authority Ltd ex p Insurance services plc 1989** and **R v Bar Council ex p Percival** that as a general rules, regulatory authorities would be considered as performing a 'public function'. The rationale for this being that if the industry was no self-regulated, then Parliament would almost certainly need to intervene in the regulation of the activity. While seemingly clear, some regulatory authorities, such as the Football Association in **R v Football Association ex P Football League 1993,** have been considered to not be subject to JR. This may seem confusing however it was explained as not being capable of JR on the basis that despite compulsory membership being needed for regulation, it was not compulsory for potential members to join the Football Association to practice in that particular field (i.e the Football League is capable of choosing whether it should join or not).

We can further establish that as per **R v Chief Rabbi of the United Hebrew Congregation of GB and Commonwealth ex p Wachmann 1993**, religious groups are also not considered to be performing a "public function" and so are not subject to JR.

It is understandable that public bodies should be accountable for the decisions they make and some form of appeal needs to be available. Our current legal system provides that the processes of public authorities and officials can be scrutinised by the mechanism of JR. In it's current form, JR is the product of a change in the attitudes of the judiciary and was led by **Lord Reid** in **Ridge v Baldwin 1964** where he decided that a public decision would be accountable on the basis of it meeting strict specifications.

Prerogative powers

It was famously decided in **Council of Civil Service Unions v Minister for the Civil Service** [1985] that a prerogative power may by subject to JR dependent on the subject matter; such as this instance where by allowing the decision of the government to remove the right to strike from workers of the SIS, as a process of national security, and further establishing the circumstances on which this may be achieved. This was further clarified in **R v Secretary for Foreign and Commonwealth Affairs ex p Everett [1989]** by **Taylor, LJ** who stated that *"The majority of their*

Lordships indicated that whether the judicial review of the exercise of prerogative power is open depends upon the subject matter and in particular whether it is justiciable. At the top of the scale of executive functions under the prerogative are matters of high policy, of which examples were given by their Lordships; making treaties, making war, dissolving Parliament ... clearly those matters ... are not justiciable. But the grant or refusal of a passport is in a quite different category. It is a matter of administrative decision affecting the rights of individuals an their freedom to travel".

The procedural restrictions of judicial review

It is important to ensure that the public bodies responsible for the governance of the state are afforded the necessary power to fulfil their responsibilities with as little restriction as can be given. To ensure that applications for JR remain limited and that the process is managed as timely as is possible there have been a number of conditions placed upon the application process.

The claim must involve a 'Public Body'

As above, the decision in dispute must be that under the definition of a 'public body'; this is largely defined by the principles set out in the aforesaid case of **R v Panel of Takeovers and Mergers ex p Datafin** and includes the principles applied in **R v Criminal Injuries Compensation Board Ex p Lain** where it was held by the High Court that a decision made concerning public funds would also be considered to be a public body for the application of JR.

The claim is made within three months of the decision in dispute

There is a time limit directed by the **Civil Procedure Rules (CPR) part 45.5(4)** as "a claim must be filed promptly and no later than 3 months". In contract to a *normal* civil claim, the parties may not opt for this to be extended however the Court may exercise its power under **CPR Part 31**. It is likely that as per **R v Dairy Produce Quota Tribunal ex p Carswell [1990]**, unless the justification for the delay is clear then the Courts will use this opportunity to refuse permission.

The claimant has sufficient interest in the case

For a claim to be brought for JR it must be established that the claimant must have sufficient **locus standi,** or standing, as provided by **Section 31(3) Supreme Court Act 1981 (Part 54 CPR)** as "…the court shall not grant leave unless it considers that applicant has sufficient interest in the matter to which the application relates". The leading decision for interpretation of the 'sufficient interest' test was given in **IRC v National Federation of Self-Employed and Small Businesses [1982]** where the House of Lords defined the process below.

In claims that involve individuals, the common question of application is that the individual should be directly affected by the decision in question; as held by **R v Secretary of State for Home Department ex p Venables [1998],** cases concerning an individual, in this instance a sentence of imprisonment, will be applicable for JR. Of direct importance to the aforesaid case, and in contrast, it was held in **R v Secretary of State for the Home Department ex p Bulger [2001]** that the father of the victim of murder did not have a direct interest; the two parties with an interest in criminal cases are the Crown and the defendant.

There are circumstances concerning the claims of 'pressure and interest groups', that allow a claim for JR by an individual entity; a restrictive view was formally taken by the High Court in **R v Secretary of State for the Enviroment ex p Rose Theatre Trust Co Ltd [1990]** where it was held that the interest group campaigning to have an archaeological site 'listed' did not satisfy the necessity for individual standing. This decision has been criticised in more recent cases such as **R v Secretary of State for the Environment ex p Greenpeace Ltd [1994]** on which permission to apply was granted to challenge a variation to the nuclea processing licence. Following this, groups further pressured their right to stand; it was stated by **Rose LJ** in **R v Secretary of States for Foreign and Commonwealth Affairs ex p World Development Movement Ltd [1995]** that circumstances contribution to the decision included 'the importance of vindicating the rule of law; the likely absence of any other responsible challenger; the nature of the breach of duty against which relief was sought; and the prominent role of the applicants in giving advice, guidance and assistance on overseas aid'. More recent developments have allowed the Courts to become more liberal in considering standing; it was held in **Equal Opportunities Commission v Secretary of State for Employment [1994]** that a group may contain a number of individuals on the provision that it involved 'matters of public importance', in this instance that of sexual discrimination.

A further variant of standing is that if **Section 6 Human Rights Act 1998** is granted to an individual or group under **Section 7 Human Rights Act 1998** as a 'victim', this can be seen in **Director of Fair Trading v Propriety Association of Great Britain [2001]** where the trade association for manufacturers was held not to be a victim.

All other methods of challenging the decision have been exhausted

While **Section 31(3) Supreme Court Act 1981** and **Part 53 CPR** fails to make adequate interpretation of whethera claimant would have a discretion of whether to pursue a civil claim or apply for JR; The House of Lords attempted to clarify the positions within **O'Reilly v Mackman [1983] 2 AC** where it established the general procedure rule that JR was the **exclusive** procedure for challenging public law decisions; and, in **Cocks v Thanet DC [1982] 3 All ER 1135** where the House of Lords decided that, in the case of a local authority's duty to house homeless people, cases could be divided into separate issues, one of which is applicable through JR and one which is not. Further to this, **Lord Diplock** held that there would be two exceptions to this rules; firstly that **Order 53** need not be used when neither party objects to the use of private law procedure and finally in instances where the claim arises out of some other legal claim, this can be seen in **Roy v Kensington and Chelsea and Westminster Family Practitioner Committee (FPC) [1992]** where it was decided that a Doctor who was working for the NHS received payment as a statutory right however the FPC has a discretionary power to reduce the payment if they considered that a GP was 'not devoting substantial time to his NHS work'; on appeal to the House of Lords it was decided by unanimous decision that *"an issue, which was concerned exclusively with public right, should be determined in judicial* *review proceedings. However, where a litigant was asserting a private law right, which incidentally involved the examination of a public law issue (the FPC's decision), he was not debarred from seeking to establish that right by ordinary action. Dr Roy had a bundle of private law rights, including the right to be paid for work done, which entitled him to sue for their alleged breach. It was not an abuse of the process of the court to proceed as Dr Roy had done",* **Lord Lowry** went on to suggest that flexibility must be maintained to avoid the striking out of genuine claims through abuse of process when it was foreseeable to suggest that a claimant use that route of claim. This decision was criticised however was used in **Mercury Communications Ltd v Director-General of Telecommunications [1996]** for the House of Lords to define the position as 'retaining flexibility about the precise limits of public and private law', their Lordships believed that the overriding consideration was for the Court to ask whether the proceedings constitute and abuse of process. **Lord Woolf** eliminated all remaining ambiguity in **The Trustee of Dennis Rye Pension Fun v Sheffield City Council [1998]** by stating that if an applicant was unsure of which route to use then JR should be favoured and that the courts always have the power to transfer a case if deemed necessary.

Permission must be granted

Prior to bringing a claim under JR, the claimant must seek permission from the High Court, as defined in **IRC v National Federation of Self-Employed and Small Businesses [1982]** this is a test of establishing whether or not the prima facie case has substance to endure a main hearing; it is described as being used to turn away 'hopeless or meddlesome applicants'. As in **Roy v Kensington and Chelsea and Westminster Family Practitioner Committee (FPC) [1992]**, it is at this stage that the case will be scrutinised against the aforesaid criteria.

Judicial review as a remedy

The applicant for JR may seek one or more of a number of remedies; a quashing order to quash the impugned decision; a prohibitory order to prevent a public body from acting or continuing to act ultra vires; a mandatory order compelling the public body to perform a duty; a declaration to confirm a legal position; an injunction to order a party to perform or refrain from performing a specific act.

Limitations of Judicial review

Restrictions within the application of JR are primarily concerned with the Courts power to amend a decision as seen in **R v Monopolies and Mergers Commission Ex P Argyll Group Plc** where it was decided that the decision in question, while applicable to the JR process, was one to be made at the discretion of the Commission itself with consent of the Secretary of State and not by virtue of JR thus the challenging of a discretionary decision of a public body is only possible if the body has acted ultra vires.

Ouster clauses

Exclusion clauses, colloquially referred to as 'ouster clauses', can often be found within the terms of public bodies however the courts are generally hostile towards them as it can be said that they are a challenge to the rule of law. The leading case in this area is **Anisminic v Foreign Compensation Commission (FCC) [1969]** where the House of Lords held that the ouster clause did not prevent the claimant from challenging a decision of the FCC. This was challenged by controversy within an attempt to oust the jurisdiction of the Administrative Court by the **Asylum and Immigration Tribunal** with use of the **Asylum and Immigration (Treatment of Claimants etc) Act 2004** however it was decided that the bill would be amended to remove this clause.

A further statutory ouster clause one that sets a specific time limit on which to make a JR claim; this can be seen in **Smith v East Ellow RDC [1956]** where it was decided by the House of Lords that this could only be applicable where there was a "valid practical and public policy reason". Another route in order to invalidate the provision of an ouster clause is on the grounds that it, as per **Article 6 HRA 1998**, interferes with the right to a fair trial.

Conclusion

It is clear that in light of the precedent surrounding the application of JR that the process of application has evolved from a largely ambiguous guide to a largely settled process.

Chapter 16 – Grounds of Judicial Review: Illegality

Question

'The prerogative – a paradox in a modern democratic state – is likely to retain its uncertain form, thus leaving to government a residue of largely uncontrolled power.' - Hilaire Barnett

Examine the meaning of the prerogative and the extent to which prerogative powers are controlled under the UK Constitution.

Answer

Introduction

In this essay we will discuss the prerogative powers exercised by the executive and the controls in place to limit that exercise being (A) the role of courts to determine extent and existence of the prerogative (B) judicial review (C) parliamentary controls and (D) reform.

The royal prerogative

Many powers are exercised by ministers and officials under primary or secondary legislation but the royal prerogative refers to those powers which have been left over from the period when the monarch was directly involved in the process of government.
As the government of the realm became more complex, power was devolved from the monarch and exercised by his/her advisers. These powers exercised by ministers include: making treaties, declaring war, deploying armed forces, regulating the civil service and granting royal pardons (amongst others). Dicey defines the royal prerogative as 'the residue of discretionary or arbitrary authority which at any given time is legally left in the hands of the Crown.'

The royal prerogative is residual in that judges will not add to the monarch's powers and that these powers can be taken away by statute. Discretionary and arbitrary mean that the monarch cannot be held accountable in the courts for the exercise of these powers. The Crown means either monarch or executive. Blackstone describes the prerogative slightly differently as those powers that 'the king enjoys alone, in contradistinction to others, and not to those he enjoys with in common with any of his subjects.' In Attorney General v De Keyser's Royal Hotel Ltd (1920), Lord Dunedin accepted Dicey's definition whereas as Lord Parmoor in the same case favoured Blackstone's notion of the prerogative powers being exclusive in nature.

Scope

The scope of the royal prerogative is difficult to determine but its existence and the extent of its power is a matter of common law making the courts the final arbiter of whether or not a particular type of prerogative power exists. In the Case of Proclamation (1610), Chief Justice Coke noted 'the king hath no prerogative but that which the law of the land allows him.' It established the monarch could only make laws through parliament and began to set out the principle when a case involving an alleged exercise of prerogative power came before the courts, the courts could determine (i) whether the prerogative existed in law and how far it extended; and (ii) whether it had been limited by statute and if so in what way.

The difficulty is that there are many prerogative powers for which there is either no recent judicial authority or no judicial authority at all. In such circumstances reliance is made on previous government practice and legal textbooks, the most comprehensive of which is now nearly 200 years old! (Joseph Chitty's, A Treatise on the Law of the Prerogatives of the Crown (1820)). Professor Brazier has noted in Constitutional Reform and the Crown (1999) that 'the demand for a statement of what may be done by virtue of the royal prerogative is of practical importance. Yet it has been said judicially (by Nourse LJ) such a statement cannot be arrived.....'

(A) The role of courts to determine extent and existence of the prerogative

(i)   Statutory powers prevail over the prerogative (and there is a suggestion that where the statutory provision covers the same ground as the prerogative, the prerogative is suspended and may only be re-activated if the statute is repealed): This was shown in Attorney General v De Keyser's Royal Hotel Ltd (1920) when the government took over a hotel under prerogative power in wartime and denied compensation due under the Defence Act 1842. The courts overrode the prerogative and held that compensation to the hotel owners was due.

(ii)   The courts should neither broaden nor expand the scope of prerogative authority: In British Broadcasting Corporation v Johns (1965), the BBC argued that it was immune from tax as it had been created under Royal Charter and broadcast under terms agreed with a Minister of the Crown. The CoA rejected this argument with Lord Diplock stating it was '350 years and a civil war too late for the Queen's courts to broaden the prerogative.....'

(iii)   Statutory powers and prerogative powers can exist in parallel without inconsistency in so far as a prerogative power exists but has not been used: In R v Secretary of State for the Home Department ex parte Northumbria Police Authority (1989) a police authority challenged the legality of a decision made by the Home Secretary to allow police chief constables access to CS gas and plastic bullets without the consent of the local police authority [under the Police Act 1964 police authorities are to provide equipment to their local forces; something which conflicted with the prerogative]. The CoA held the Home Secretary's decision could be justified under both statute and prerogative (under the prerogative powers to keep the peace within the realm)[180].

(iv)   It is an abuse of power for the executive to use the royal prerogative to achieve something inconsistent with a statutory scheme or frustrate the will of parliament expressed in statute: In R v Secretary of State for the

---

[180] There has been some criticism of this decision by Robert Ward as there is no authority for the view that the prerogative power of keeping the peace extends to arming police with CS gas and plastic bullets; and therefore looks like the 'recognition of a new prerogative.'

Home Department ex p Fire Brigades Union (1995), the HoL ruled that the Home Secretary had acted unlawfully by introducing a lower rate of compensation for compensating victims of crime (which several members of various unions would have been subject to) under his prerogative powers. In doing so the Home Secretary had by-passed a statutory scheme which had been approved by parliament but not yet activated.

(v)   A prerogative power could not be used to defeat a statutory right granted by an act of parliament: In Laker Airways v Department of Trade (1977), the court rejected the government's argument that it had the right under the prerogative to deny Laker Airway's; a previously given right, to fly a transatlantic route.

(B) Judicial review

(i)   The exercise of prerogative powers maybe subject to judicial review depending on the justiciability of the of the subject matter [Lord Roskill noted that certain exercises of the prerogative are non-justiciable (not subject to trial in court) and these are: making of treaties, defence of the realm, prerogative of mercy, granting of honours and appointment of ministers]: In Council of Civil Service Unions v Minister for the Civil Service (1985) (the GCHQ case), the Minister for the civil service relied on the royal prerogative to alter terms and conditions of service such that no civil staff at GCHQ could belong to a trade union and therefore take part in strike action. It was noted that any enforcement order by exercise of the royal prerogative could be subject to judicial review.

(ii)   Prerogative legislation (orders in council) could be subject to judicial review. In R (Bancoult) v Secretary of State for Foreign and Commonwealth Affairs (No.2), it was noted that the Crown has no prerogative power to exclude British subjects from their territory. This suggests the courts are now more willing to judicially review prerogative acts when they infringe human rights and are less concerned that some areas are out of bounds (as compared to Lord Roskill's non-justiciable view in the GCHQ case).

(C) Parliamentary controls

(i)   Legislate: parliament can legislate to modify, abolish or put on a statutory footing any particular prerogative power. For example the Civil Contingencies Act 2004 covers the majority of situations where previously the royal prerogative (as noted in the Case of the King's prerogative in Salt petre (1606)) could have been used to take and destroy private property to stop it falling into enemy hands.

(ii)   Accountability to parliament: ministers are accountable to parliament for all their actions including those taken under the prerogative powers. This may also include scrutiny by Departmental Select Committees.

(iii) Parliamentary approval of expenditure: parliamentary approval is required where the use of prerogative involves the incurring of expenditure.

(iv)   Initiation of an enquiry: The Inquiries Act 2005 provides a minister can launch an enquiry if it appears that particular events have caused or are capable of causing public concern.

(D) Reform

The Fixed Term Parliaments Act 2011 abolishes the royal prerogative of dissolution and provides that general elections will be at fixed 5 year intervals. The Constitutional Reform and Governance Act 2010 subjects the prerogative treaty making power to a requirement that treaties be laid before parliament for 21 days (thereby placing the 'Ponsonby rule' on a statutory footing) before they can be ratified.

The regulation of the civil service was historically achieved under the royal prerogative but the Constitutional Reform and Governance Act 2010 places the power to manage the civil service on a statutory basis. A 2007 consultation paper asked whether the prerogative power to send British troops into armed combat should be placed on a statutory basis. The approach emerging was for the requirement that the PM must provide information to parliament as to a proposed deployment in advance of the deployment and for a deployment to be subject to authorisation by the commons. An example of this occurring is the PM giving parliament this information in a debate about Libya on 21 March 2011 following which deployment was approved.

However a key problem arising in placing statutory controls over prerogative powers is that the flexibility in dealing with certain circumstances is extinguished resulting in either inflexibility or a very broad statutory power.

Conclusion

To a varying extent there are political and legal controls over the exercise of prerogative powers, with reform in the area putting certain powers on a statutory footing. Prerogative powers represent one of the most fundamentally significant areas of constitution law, not least because of their definitional difficulties. However, the most controversial aspect remains controlling their use. Prerogative powers have developed into a significant source of the UK constitution. Like most of the other type of elements that make the constitution, it is not enlisted as a formal text in any single document and may appear less constructive. However, when it comes to the definition of Prerogative powers, Dicey's offering in this matter is not hard to grasp – '... *the residue of discretionary or arbitrary authority, which at any time is legally left in the hands of the Crown ... Every act which the executive government can lawfully do without the authority of an Act of Parliament is done in virtue of this prerogative[181].* ' With regards to Blackstones[182] and Joseph Chitty's[183] definition of the prerogative and Dicey's version

---

[181] [1885, p 424] – Constitutional & Administrative Law, Fifth Edition, Hilaire Barnett, Cavendish Publishing, chp6, p 124

[182] *Commentaries* (1765-69) by Blackstone define Prerogative powers as – *'that special pre-eminance whicht the King hath over and above all other persons....'*

[183] Joseph Chitty [1820, p2] defines Prerogative power as *'the rights of*

provides us the following –

- Prerogative powers are inherent and exclusive to the Crown
- It is a production of Common Law and these powers are residual ie pertaining from other law
- These powers are commonly and widely used by the Executive for the Crown
- Exercise of Prerogative powers do not require authority from an Act of Parliament

The Courts can also impliedly render a prerogative suspended by relying or giving way to a more appropriate statute provision. In *De Keyser's*[184] the Crown's discretionary power to award compensation to those affected by the emergency seizure of properties in course of the defence of the realm, was suspended by a more generous compensation scheme provided by a relevant statute. In limiting the Executive's exercise of prerogative powers, the Courts have also held ministerial advice given to the Crown, up for review when that advice was based on an error of law in *ex parte Bently*[185].

Prerogative powers have best suited its application at times of grave emergency. These set of powers are designed to properly apply and respond to a vast possible number of situations may be previously unseen and unprecedented. With the above control measures in place it is for the betterment of transparent accountable democracy that scrutiny and controlling mechanisms are in place. And it is perhaps for the greater good that these historical, unique powers are delegated from the Crown and also retained by the Crown exclusively in appropriate arrangement of the modern British Constitution.

---

sovereignty........distinct from the people at large'
[184] A.-G. v. De Keyser's Royal Hotel [1920] AC 508
[185] R. v. Home Secretary, ex p. Bentley [1994] QB 349

Chapter 17 - Unreasonableness/Irrationality and Proportionality

Question

'I think that the day will come when it will be more widely recognised that [Wednesbury] was an unfortunately retrogressive decision in English administrative law, insofar as it suggested that there are degrees of unreasonableness and that only a very extreme degree can bring an administrative decision within the legitimate scope of judicial invalidation' (per Lord Cooke in **R v Secretary of State for the Home Department, ex parte Daly** (2001)).

Discuss.

Introduction

In this paper we will discuss the impact of Wednesbury unreasonableness within the scope of English administrative law; to do this we will look at the below points.

1. Unreasonableness
2. Wednesbury unreasonableness
3. Irrationality
4. Wednesbury test within classes of unreasonableness
5. Decisions affecting fundamental rights
6. Reform / conclusion

Unreasonableness

One ground of challenge in judicial review is that of the public body having acted unreasonably; this definition summary of this is laid out in **Roberts v Hopwood [1925]** as 'A person... must, by the use of his reason, ascertain and follow the course which reason directs. He must act reasonably".

Wednesbury unreasonableness

Following the above, and, a decision by the Court of Appeal in **Associated Provincial Picture Houses Ltd v Wednesbury Corporation [1947]**, it became known as 'Wednesbury unreasonableness', because; Lord Greene MR reviewed existing case law and attempted to summarise what he considered to be well-established principles. He pointed out that the courts authority was not to interfere with policy that it may feel is unreasonable however it is able to interfere where it deems that the local authority had acted unreasonably in **'a decision on a competent matter is so unreasonable that no reasonable authority could ever have come to'**; it was made clear that this would require something overwhelming. Unfortunately, Lord Greene did not discuss in any great depth what would be so unreasonable that no reasonable authority could ever have come to it.

Irrationality

The Wednesbury test was further evolved by Lord Diplock in the case of **GCHQ** where he preferred to use the term 'irrationality' to describe 'unreasonableness', he explained that "It applies to a decision which is so outrageous in its defiance of logic or accepted moral standards that no sensible person who had applied his mind to the question to be decided could have arrived at it." The difficulty lays in whether 'unreasonableness' and 'irrationality' are entirely the same. In **R v Devon CC ex p G [1988]**, Lord Donaldson MR stated that he preferred to use the old term 'Wednesbury unreasonableness' and he suggested that 'the imprimatur of Lord Diplock in (GCHQ) is widely misunderstood by politicians …. as casting doubt on the mental capacity of the decision-maker, a matter which in practice is seldom, if ever, an issue.'

Lord Cooke went on further to, as in **R v Chief Constable of Sussex ex p International Traders Ferry [1999]**, describe Lord Greene's formulation as tautologous and exaggerated; his preference was simply to ask the question of whether the decision in question was 'one which a reasonable authority could reach'. The difficulty here is that due to the largely ambiguous Wednesbury test, the judiciary has separated in their interpretation of the law to ensure that justice is done.

Wednesbury test within classes of unreasonableness

While the Wednesbury test is to be applied to a decision of the local authority, it must also be applied within a number of classes of unreasonableness, that is, the types of unreasonableness that have been identified by the courts must still apply the Wednesbury test. These can be found in **De Smith & Jowell** where it was outlined that the three main classes are Material defects in decision-making process, oppressive decisions and Violations of constitutional principles. It is worth noting that the Wednesbury test has been applied in these instances with, at the very least, moderate success.

Material defects in the decision-making process

The first circumstance will be where it can be proven that there were material defects in the decision-making process, that is, where the local authority has either wrongly weighed up relevant factors or where a decision-maker fails to provide a comprehensible chain of reasoning for the decision. This can be seen in **West Glamorgan CC v Rafferty [1987]** where it was decided that travellers facing eviction from local authority land had successfully argued that the action would be unreasonable because the local authority was under a statutory duty to provide sites in their area and had failed to do this, and, in **R v Secretary of State for the Home Department ex p Cox [1993]** where it was decided, based on the Wednesbury test, that a convicted murderer who was released on licence would be recalled to prison to serve two further years after being arrested and charged with a minor offence, it was decided that the Secretary of State had failed to give sufficient weight to the length of detention.

Oppressive decisions

The second circumstance is when a decision is considered 'oppressive' within its nature. This can be seen in **Wheeler v Leicester City Council [1985]** where it was decided to be Wednesbury unreasonable for the local authority to remove the use of the rugby club's training grounds because they had several players whom were planning to play in South Africa.

Violation of constitutional principles

Finally, decisions that are proved to be arbitrary in nature may lead to inquiry; this can be seen in **r v Secretary of State for the Home Department ex p McCartney [1994]** where it was considered to be Wednesbury unreasonable for the Home Secretary to sentence the defendant to three life sentences for the attempted murder of a policeman while convictions of more serious crimes were sentenced more leniently.

Decisions affecting fundamental rights

It was first noted in **Bugdaycay v Secretary of State for the Home Department [1987]** that the Courts must perform and increasingly intensive review in circumstances affecting a persons basic human rights. This was further reported in **R v Ministry of Defence ex p Smith [1996]** where Sir Thomas Bingham MR stated that *"the more substantial the interference with human rights, the more th court will require by way of justification before it is satisfied that the decision is reasonable in the sense that it is within the range of reasons open to a reasonable decision-maker"*. Thus the level of inquiry naturally heightened in comparison to the largely ambiguous Wednesbury test.

The **Human Rights Act 1998** has significantly amended the *normal* use of the Wednesbury test by introducing a test of **proportionality** in decisions relating to a person's fundamental rights. A good illustration of this change can be seen in **R v Secretary of State for the Home Department ex p Daly [2001]**, where the Court stated that there were: 'material differences between the Wednesbury and Smith grounds of review and the approach of proportionality is applicable in respect of review where Convention rights are at stake'. This, along with the more recent decision in **R v Swindon NHS Primary Care Trust & Secretary of State for Health [2006]**, has helped redefine the Wednesbury test however this does only extent as far as cases concerning Article 2 of the Human Rights Act 1998.

Reform / conclusion

The difficulty in large reform of the current law concerning the Wednesbury test is that current precedent is now largely settled, however; introduction of the application of the Human Rights Act 1998 in 2000 has caused a necessary interpretation of the Wednesbury test to include a more rigorous test of justification in circumstances concerning Article 2.

While it seems certain that even if it were to be considered that the Wednesbury test be a regression in English administrative law, the Courts have used their power of interpretation to settle the law in this area concerning decisions of the public authority, of course, reasonableness also extends to the practicalities of the court in modern day.

The Wednesbury test however has been widely criticized within the judiciary with **Lord Ackner** stating that *"Unless and until Parliament incorporates the convention into domestic law...there appears to me to be at present no basis upon which the proportionality doctrine applied by the European Court can be followed by the Courts of this country..."*. Further to this, in the case of **Daly** itself, **Lord Cooke** stated that

"The day will come when it will be more widely recognised that ... Wednesbury ... was an unfortunately retrogressive decision in English administrative law ... in so far as it suggested that there are degrees of unreasonableness and that only a very extreme degree can bring an administrative decision within the legitimate scope of judicial invalidation. ... The depth of judicial review and the deference due to administrative discretion vary with the subject matter. It may well be, however, that the law can never be satisfied in any administrative field merely by finding that the decision under review is not capricious or absurd."

It was further suggested in **R v Secretary of State for the Environment, Transport and Religions [2001]** that proportionality and Wednesbury were conflicting tests that made it difficult for the judiciary to adequately enforce their legal obligations.

It is perhaps overlooks that the fundamental advantage of the Wednesbury test, in its current form, is that it is effectively acting as a 'flood gate' for cases wishing to challenge the local authority through judicial review. While it is important that justice be done, it is also worth noting that Court reform (in the form of CPR etc) has brought our courts into a respectable state. It is possible that a move to proportionality would move the Courts back into a Dickensian era.

Chapter 18 – Procedural impropriety

Problem Question 1

In order to combat what is seen as an undesirable growth in broadcast content which is seen as 'unsuitable', Parliament has enacted the (fictitious) Films (Undesirable Content) Act 2012. The Act is notable for a number of its provisions, including:

Section 1, which allows the Secretary of State for Culture, Media and Sport to prohibit the showing of films if the content of such a film is deemed to be "unsuitable for showing to the general public on grounds of taste and decency".

Section 2, which requires the Secretary of State for Culture, Media and Sport to draw up a Code of Conduct for film producers. This Code of Conduct should offer guidance to film producers and cinemas as to the material which might be considered to be unsuitable for the purposes of section 1. The provision is notable in that it places the Secretary of State under a duty to draw up the Code of Conduct "after consultation with those parties who will be affected".

Section 3, which permits the Secretary of State for Culture, Media and Sport to levy fines or serve a 'closure order' on cinemas which show films which contravene the Code of Conduct. A 'closure order' might apply either for a limited period or could be imposed on a permanent basis.

These provisions are now in force and have been in operation for a few months. As a result of the operation of these provisions a number of people come to you for advice.

Advise the following parties **both in relation to potential claims for judicial review and any other possible remedies** which might arise from the following circumstances:

1. A famous film director, Tintin Quarantino, comes to see you because his latest film has been prohibited under the powers given to the Secretary of State in section 1 of the Films (Undesirable Content) Act 2012. Tintin admits that his films are known for their

"challenging" content, both in terms of violence and sexual portrayal, but he does not feel that his latest film is any more graphic than his previous productions. The only reason that Tintin has been given for the prohibition is that his latest film is 'unsuitable'. He comes to you seeking advice on the best course of action to take in order to get the prohibition lifted.

2. The National Association of Cinema Operators, a trade body representing independent cinema owners, also seeks your advice. The Association was identified as an 'affected party' for the purposes of section 2 of the Act. The Association was sent a 210 page consultation document on the proposals for the Code of Conduct and given a time limit for responses of 5 working days. The Association was most concerned to discover that the Secretary of State had published a draft Code of Conduct before the expiration of the 5 working day deadline and that the final Code of Conduct does not seem to have been altered in any way from the text of the draft. The Association are disappointed by the Secretary of State's actions in their case and wish to know whether there is any possibility of challenging the Code of Conduct.

3. Scott Ridley, a film producer, contacts you after dealing with a senior civil servant in the government department which created the Code of Conduct. Scott wishes to produce a new film and he is unsure whether or not certain parts of the film are likely to be compatible with the Code of Conduct. In an attempt to clarify his position, Scott wrote to the department 10 weeks ago seeking clarification of a number of points in the Code but did not receive a response. As a result of this, Scott telephoned the government department and spoke to a senior civil servant, who said that they had lost his original letter and that, furthermore, the department would not 'waste time' offering advice on the interpretation of the Code of Conduct. Scott is both aggrieved and upset about his treatment and wonders whether there are any means of redress available to him.

4. Cinemascape, a cinema company owned by Phil Projector. In a recent incident, 3 of Cinemascape's 55 cinemas accidentally showed an un-edited version of a film which had three minutes of prohibited footage which should have been edited out. The mistake was quickly noticed and the film was only shown on one occasion

at each of the three cinemas. The Secretary of State has responded to this by issuing a closure order, closing all 55 of Cinemascape's cinemas for four weeks and levying a fine of £500,000. This has caused substantial damage to Cinemascape's business and the company now runs the risk of insolvency due to the lost revenue resulting from the closure of its cinemas. Phil wishes to know what options may be available to him to challenge the measures taken against Cinemascape and to seek some recompense for the heavy losses that have been incurred due to the closures.

Answer

1) Tintin Quarantino faces a situation where his latest film has been prohibited under Section 1 of the Films Act 2012. However there are three legal issues on the basis of which the prohibition could be lifted. Namely; the inclusion of Duty to give a reason, the freedom of expression/proportionality of legislation and the principle of legitimate expectation.

Duty to give Reasons

The 1932 report on Minister's powers, referring to decisions by ministers and tribunals said 'Any party affected by a decision should be informed of the reasons on which the decision is based...in the form of a reasoned document'[186] this was reaffirmed in the Franks Report 1957. This can be linked to the situation Tintin is facing having only been provided with the reason that his film is 'unsuitable.' Without stating the grounds for their conclusion. In the Case of Alexander Machinery Ltd v Crabtree[187] Sir John Donaldson stated failure to give adequate reasons may amount to an error of law so as to justify the quashing of the decision.

Another stance Tintin could take is that the Secretary of State has in fact given no real reason having simply quoted 'unsuitable' from the Section 1 of the Films Act 2012. In Padfield v Minister of Agriculture[188] Lord Upjohn said if a minister did not give any reasons for a decision 'it may be, if the circumstances warrant it,

---

[186] CMD 4060 Folkes Administrative Law Sixth Edition Butterworths
[187] [1974] ICR 120
[188] [1968] AC 997, [1968] 1 All ER 694

that a court may be at liberty to come to the conclusion that he had no good reason for reaching that conclusion and directing a prerogative order to be issued accordingly'.[189] However we're not yet moving to a position where there's an absolute statutory duty to give a reason, nevertheless Woolf J said that 'decisions had at least to make clear to the parties his reasons that led to his conclusion'[190]. The case of R v Social Security Commissioner[191] said that the absence or the inadequacy of reasons may have reasons other than litigation, such as the award of cost against the authority or even a matter for criticism by an Ombudsman. There is no express requirement to give reasons at common law, so the justifiability of Tintin taking this action is risky, nevertheless the ECtHR regards this as implicit in the obligation to provide a fair hearing. Reasons do not have to be given on every single point, but they must be sufficient to enable a party to understand the essence of the decision. [192]

Legitimate expectation

The second legal issue as defence to the Secretary of State ruling is legitimate expectation, Lord Diplock stated in GCHQ it "must affect the other person...by depriving him of some benefit or advantage which he had in the past been permitted by the decision maker to which he can legitimately expect to be permitted to continue..."

Tintin previous films (approved) are known for their "challenging" content. Tintin doesn't believe that his latest film is any more graphic than his previous productions. Whether this past practice of approval can be legitimately expected to continue, in this instance, a matter of implied representation.

Freedom of expression

Finally Tintin could argue, with the introduction of the Films Act

---

[189]Fn.2above, at 1061 and 719

[190] Greenfell-Baines v Secretary of State for the Enviroment [1985] JPL 256.

[191] 1985 Times, 2 January

[192] Helle v Finland 1998) 26E.H.R.R 159

2012, is a breach of his freedom of expression and the right to hold opinions and impact information without interference by a public authority protected under Article 10 ECHR. Expression is broadly defined and includes artistic and commercial expression[193]. It also protects speech which shocks, offends or disturbs. The argument of whether the legislation imposed by the Secretary of State is a disproportionate restriction on Tintin's freedom of expression, then the best route for Tintin would be to challenge under section 7 of the HRA 1998. *Section* 7 of the HRA 1998 allows Tintin to seek redress in the European Court of Human Rights.

Remedy

Having established a lack of reasons provided by the Secretary of State and to some extent no real reason at all, it would be advisable for Tintin to seek Judicial review against the Secretary of State based on the arguments in order to have the prohibition lifted or quashed. Whether standing has been fulfilled is unquestionable as Tintin's rights have been directly affected.

2) The National Association of Cinema operators are seeking to challenge the Code of Conduct imposed recently by the Secretary of State, my view is that the most convincing route to take in order to seek Judicial Review is on the basis of inadequate consultation. Although there's no general duty to consult imposed by the common law where the order is of a legislative nature, it's been held in the case of Aylesbury Mushrooms[194], the duty to consult is 'invariably mandatory' and under Section 2 of the 2012 Act of this case consultation must be given to "...those parties who will be affected."

What approach courts take to determine whether adequate consultation has taken place is evident in the Gunning Criteria[195] which states: that the consultation is at a time when proposals are still at a formative stage, that the proposer gives sufficient reasons for any proposals to permit intelligent consideration and response, thirdly that adequate time has been given for consideration and

---

[193] Wingrove v Uk [1996] 24 E.H.R.R 1, paras 47-50
[194] Aylesbury Mushrooms Ltd [1972] 1 WLR 190
[195] [1985] 84 LGR 168

response, finally the responses are taken into account.

In this particular case we are concerned with the third and fourth points in the Gunning Criteria[196]. First of which states 'that adequate time must be given for consideration and response', whether a time limit for responses of 5 working days is "adequate" is debatable. In the case of Lee[197], the Minister by law was bound to give school governors an opportunity to make representations to him, he gave them four days, the court held that this was "wholly unreasonable" and extended the time by four weeks, this was seen in the Dredger[198] case where seven days was also seen as inadequate. In the case of Port Louis Corp it was stated that 'adequate time'[199] was whether there was reasonable time to express views on a clear proposal. Taking these past case laws into account, it seems unreasonable that 5 days is enough to read and thoroughly analyse a 210 page consultation document.

Furthermore 'the product of the consultation must be conscientiously taken into account in finalising statutory proposals'. This is unfounded in this particular case where the draft code was published before the 5 day deadline and the final Code of Conduct having seemingly been unaltered from the text in the draft, despite the legal obligation under section 2 of the 2012 Act. The opinions and views expressed must be considered with an open and, as Morris J had put it, a 'receptive' mind. Failure to do so will result in the quashing of the decision as seen in the case of R v Manchester Metropolitan University[200].

Having established from the Gunning Criteria[201] that the consultation procedure implemented by the Secretary of State was far from adequate, the best cause of action for 'The Association' is a claim for judicial review, dependant on the criteria of standing and time limits, applicable to all four questions when seeking for

---

[196] [1985] 84 LGR 168
[197]
[198] [1993] C.O.D
[199] R v Secretary of State for Education and Employment [2000] Ed. CR. 603
[200] Ex P Nolan, The Independent, July 15th 1993.
[201] [1985] 84 LGR 168

judicial review. A person should possess standing when they have sufficient interest in the matter to which the application relates. The test proposed by the Law Commission has now been incorporated in the Supreme Court Act 1981 s31.The message gleamed from the IRC[202] case was that there should be a unified test of testing based upon sufficiency of interest. Standing at the leave stage however was criticised, with Sedley J holding that standing at such a stage should only be refused if it was clear that the applicant was a "busybody" with no legitimate expectation. The argument for the fusion approach was that it is only by looking at the type of injury, the aims of the legislation, and the interest affected that one can decide who should be able to claim. Regarding time limits, a claim must be brought within three months of the acclaimed injustice.

3) Scott Ridley is seeking a means of redress with a senior civil servant regarding his treatment. There are two main avenues which can be pursued by Scott, that of maladministration and misfeasance, the former is one which I will consider first.

It can be argued that Scott has been a victim of carelessness, neglect, rudeness and to some extent negligence. What has to be established is whether such actions can constitute as maladministration. Following 'The Whyatt Report' in 1961 and the recommendations imposed regarding maladministration the Parliamentary Commissioner Act 1967 was passed, appointing a Parliamentary Commissioner for Administration[203] (PCA) which has adopted the term "ombudsman". Although Maladministration hasn't been defined by the Act, a sense of what the legislature intended can be derived from the Crossman catalogue which included, 'neglect, ineptitude...delay' and much more. The PCA has defined maladministration as "sustained injustice" with the term "injustice" been given a wide interpretation not covering just injury but also '...the sense of outrage aroused by unfair or incompetent administration, even where the complainant has suffered no actual loss.'[204] It's clear that Scott has faced some sort of maladministration, from the 10 week wait with no response, the

---

[202] IRC [1982] A.C. 617 at 632-633
[203] F.Stacey, The British Ombudsman (Oxford: Clarendon, 1971)
[204] Hansard HC, Vol. 734 col.51 (October 18, 1966) (R.Crossman)

loss of his original letter and finally the blunt and rude comment that the department wouldn't "waste time" offering advice.

Establishing maladministration in Scott's case it's now the responsibility of the PCA under section 5 (1) of the Parliamentary Commissioner Act 1967 to '...investigate any action taken by or on behalf of a government department or other authority to which the act applies...'[205] where maladministration has occurred. The PCA has recently published Principles of Good Administration,[206] the six principles are intimately linked with a finding of maladministration. Three principles include "being customer focused" which covers dealing with people helpfully, promptly and sensitively. Secondly acting "fairly and proportionately" which entails treating people with respect and finally the principle of "putting things right". 'The public body should acknowledge mistakes and apologise where appropriate; put mistakes right quickly and effectively.'[207] It can be seen from these principles of good administration; the senior civil servant has not conformed in the case of Scott.

However the PCA has no formal power to award a remedy even if the Commissioner finds maladministration. Nevertheless 'the Annual Report for 2010-11 states that over 99 per cent of recommendations made during the year were accepted.'[208] Remedies available can range from the scope of an apology, reconsideration of the decision, financial compensation for loss, inconvenience or distress and finally action to prevent recurrence of the problem. It would seem logical and reasonable that Scott should be entitled to an apology for the way he was treated by the senior civil servant, secondly under the principles of good administration the senior civil servant should be "putting things right" by clarifying the number of points questioned in the code. Whether Scott is entitled to compensation is difficult to answer, Scott could argue that the 10 week period with no reply had

---

[205] Re Fletcher's Application [1970] 2 All E.R. 527n, HL.
[206] Parliamentary and Health Service Ombudsman, Principles of Good Administration (2009)
[207] Administrative Law seventh Edition Paul Craig 8-018 Page 213
[208] Parliamentary and Health Service Ombudsman, Annual Report 2010-2011

delayed the release of his film and thus a loss of revenue. However I believe this argument is far too open ended and expensive to seek judicial review, in reality an apology with the situation being rectified would suffice.

Scott could also pursue the argument of the tort of misfeasance in public office[209]. In this particular instance it regards targeted malice, where a public officer has omitted to perform an act. In the Three Rivers DC[210] case malice was taken to mean that there was some intent to injure the plaintiff and he was aware that there was a serious risk that the plaintiff would suffer loss as a result. Has the senior civil servant in this particular case refused to offer advice on the interpretation of the Code of Conduct with the intent to "injure" Scott? In Abdul Carder[211] the plaintiff alleged that he had been maliciously refused a licence, the court held, that in such a case, a damages action may lie in a tort action. However in this particular instance it seems highly unlikely to be able to prove conclusively that the senior civil servant acted in bad faith in order to cause "injury" to Scott.

4) Cinemascape has faced huge financial hardship as a result of the Secretary of State decision, it seems inevitable that Phil Projector has a case to stand upon to challenge the measures imposed, based upon the principles of proportionality and Wedensbury unreasonableness seen in the case of Associated Provincial Picture Houses Ltd[212]. It was stated by Lord Greene M.R. in this case that the decision made had to be "so unreasonable that no reasonable decision-maker could come to it" for the courts to intervene. Further expanded by Lord Diplock who preferred to use the term "irrational" which applied when "...a decision which is so outrageous in its defiance of logic or accepted moral standards..."[213].
What we can understand from the above definitions is that the

---

[209] B. Gould, "Damages as a remedy in Administrative law" (1972) 5 N.Z.U.L.R. 105
[210] Three Rivers DC v Bank of England (NO.3) [2003] 2 A.C. 1 HL
[211] David v Abdul Carder [1963] 1 W.L.R. 835; A.Bradley
[212] Associated Provincial Picture Houses Ltd v Wedensbury Corp [1948] 1 K.B. 223.
[213] [1985] A.C. 374 at 410; cf. Luby v Newcastle-under-Lyme Corp [1964] 2 Q.B 64 at 72.

courts can employ both logic and accepted moral standards as criteria by which to assess official decisions.

Recently the Wedensbury test has been "loosened" in the case of R v Coughlan[214], the court held that irrationality included decisions which were made by "flawed logic"[215] or in the case of Lord Cooke in R v Chief Constable of Sussex it stated the question should be 'was the decision one which a reasonable authority could have reached'. The question is whether the decision reached is one which is "within the range of reasonable responses open to the decision-maker"[216]. The question whether the closure of Cinemascapes premises was open to the decision maker is unfounded as under Section 3 of the Films Act 2012 states that the Secretary of State is permitted to 'serve a 'closure' order'. In the case of Balchin,[217] Sedley J held that a decision would be Wedensbury unreasonable if it disclosed an error of reasoning, this does not appear to be the case in Cinemascape, what could be questioned is the rationale and logic which was implemented to reach such severe measures. Nevertheless it would be difficult to obtain such evidence having had a justifiable and legal reason to implement such measures, it is still the case '...that the Wedensbury test can be a significant hurdle for claimants.'[218] It would be best suggested that Cinemascape apply the status of proportionality first suggested by Lord Diplock in the GCHQ[219] case juxtaposed by the hostile approach found in Brind.[220]

Proportionality can be considered as a three part analysis as seen in the case of Hickman[221] and Daly[222]which considered:

---

[214] R v North and East Devon HA ex parte Coughlan [2001] Q.B. 213 at [65]

[215] Coughlan [2001] Q.B. 213 at [65]

[216] Ala v Secretary of State for the Home Department [2003] EWCA Civ 216

[217] R v Parlimentary Commisioner for Administration, Ex p. Balchin [1997] C.O.D 146 QPD

[218] R. (J) v Special Educational Needs and Disability Tribunal (SENDIST) [2005] EWHC

[219] Council for Civil Service Unions v Minister of State for the Civil Service [1985]1 A.C. 374,410.

[220] R v Secretary of State for the Home Department, Ex p. Brind [1991] 1 A.C. 696 HL.

[221] Hickman [2007] J.R 31

"whether: (i) the legislative objective is sufficiently important to justify limiting a fundamental right; (ii) the measures designed to meet the legislative objective and rationality connected to it; (iii) the means used to impair the right or freedom are no more than is necessary to accomplish the objective".

What we are concerned with is the excessive penalties imposed. Exemplified in the case of Hook[223], a stallholder who had his licence revoked for urinating in the street, resulting in a loss of livelihood, Lord Denning struck down the case deeming it as excessive and out of proportion, seen as a recognised principle of Justice that penalties should not be excessive, as acknowledged in the Bill of Rights 1689. Having looked at past case law and the similarities between such cases as Hook[224], Man (Sugar)[225] and that of Cinemascape it seems if the proportionality test was applied it would appear the decision goes beyond what is necessary to achieve the legitimate aim and thus resulting in the penalties been struck down, it would be unjust to say that one mistake could lead to a company going into liquidation.

A rather different argument which could be taken is that Secretary of State was ultra-virus, in that he implemented both closure orders and fines. Section 3 allows allows only one of the actions available to be implemented with the significant word been 'or'. Whats more closure orders accordingly to section 3 can only be implemented on those cinemas which showed the film contravening Conduct A, in this instance only 3, not all 55 cinemas. If this is found to be the case, then the decision could be quashed on the basis that the decision was 'beyond the powers' exerted upon the Secretary of State.

Alternatively 'British courts now explicitly apply proportionality

---

[222] R v Secretary of State for the Home Department Ex p. Daly [2001] UKHL 26; [2001] 2 A.C. 532
[223] R v Barnsley MBC, Ex p. Hook [1976] 1 W.L.R 1052 CA (Civ Div) at 1057.
[224] R v Barnsley MBC, Ex p. Hook [1976] 1 W.L.R 1052 CA (Civ Div) at 1057.
[225] R v Intervention Board, Ex p. Man (Sugar) ltd [1985] E.C.R 2889.

in respect of directly effective European Community Law and, under the HRA 1998, as a structured test to evaluate compatibility with Convention rights, particularly the qualified rights under Arts 8-11.'[226] In the case of Handyside v UK[227] which concerned Article 10 Freedom of Expression in which it was stated that any material which "shock, offend, disturb that state or any sector of the population every penalty imposed must be proportionate to the legitimate aim." This is another avenue which could be pursued by Cinemascape to quash the Secretary of State's decision directly through Section 7 HRA.

---

[226] De Smiths Judical Review Sixth Edition Harry Woolf P584 11-073
[227] [1979] 1 E.H.R.R. 737 at [48]

Chapter 19 – Legitimate Expectation

Essay Question 1

The recognition of substantive legitimate expectations is to be welcomed, but the standard of review in such cases remains problematic. Discuss.

Answer

Introduction

Fairness and legal certainty are two crucial factors to be seen in decisions made by public authorities; (this is when a public body say they will do something and changes its policy and or refuses to do what they promised). The doctrine of legitimate expectations is the tool used to try to ensure public body do what they promised. The doctrine comes into play when a public authority makes a declaration regarding its policy, or the manner in which it will exercise its discretion, and then seeks to retreat from this position. Those seeking to enforce such a doctrine will naturally be people who have relied on the former promise, probably to their detriment, and often with their position now worsened due to the change in policy.

Test to be applied: The old approach

Approach 1: Hamlbe Fisheries
However there has been disagreement as to whether the doctrine is truly a valid one under English law. Indeed in **Khan**, the Home Office departed from a representation of policy as regards approval of adoption from abroad, (Pakistani family adopting a child from abroad) it was held, however, that they could only depart from such a policy following a hearing and in the overriding public interest. This approach was confirmed in **Hamlbe Fisheries**, here it was held by the court that, although the policy could be changed for the future, where an expectation had *"a legitimacy which in fairness outtops policy choice"* this would be protected by the courts, and the public authority may well be required to allow an interim period or make some kind of fair warning in order to change policy in such a way. Here it can be seen that there is a

strong emphasis upon fairness in administration. **The test** (or standard of review to be adopted by the courts) to detrmine wether to grant a breach of legitimate expectation would be to ask: was an overriding public interest in the need for the change?

Approach 2: Hargreaves
The approach taken in **Hamble Fisheries** was criticised in **Hargreaves.** Further in Hardgreves the Home Secertary changed policy on prisoners' home leave with immediate effect and here the doctrine in **Hamble Fisheries** was rejected as "heresy" and "wrong in principle". Despite such seemingly strong language, there was still doubt, Craig argues, as to whether the case really did reject the principle of substantive legitimate expectations fully, or whether there was simply not such on the facts, but that if there were, such could be protected (although notably only then to the Wednesbury principle).

In other words the court held that the policy change was a matter primarily for the Home Secretary and not for the courts. They concluded that the court could review the decision but only on the grounds of *Wednesbury* unreasonableness, i.e. whether no reasonable decision maker would have decided to change the policy retrospectively and so have frustrated the legitimate expectation. In this situation, considering this was a generalised change of policy in an important area, the decision to revoke such leave retrospectively was not deemed *Wednesbury* unreasonable.

The test (or standard of review to be adopted by the courts) to detrmine wether to grant a breach of legitimate expectation would be to ask: whether no reasonable decision maker would have decided to change the policy and so have frustrated the legitimate expectation. Less of an inquiry – a lesser review – harder to satisfy!

Test to be applied: New Approach

There was an attempt to rectify the inconsistency seen above in **Coughlan**. Here the applicant had been seriously injured in 1971 and cared for in a hospital that was considered unsuitable for modern care, so in 1993 the applicant was moved to Mardon House on the strength of a promise made by the LHA to the applicant and others that they could remain here "as long as they chose". In 1998 the LHA decided to close Mardon House, the applicant challenged this decision on the basis that the promise was breached. Finding for the applicant, the court made a distinction between three types of cases;

*Important: Laws LJ stated that the categories in Coughlan were not 'hermetically sealed' and each represented a point on a scale. Laws LJ suggested that decisions that lie within the 'macro-political' field should attract a less intrusive approach by the courts (i.e. a **Wednesbury** standard of review) and those lying outside that field a higher intensity of review.*

1. The court may decide that the public authority only needs to bear **previous policy in mind** when seeking to alter, but need do no more. The decision would only then be reviewable on Wednesbury grounds. **Hardgreeves** were of this type.

2. There was a legitimate expectation of consultation engendered by the public authority (matter of procedural expectations)

3. A lawful promise induces a legitimate expectation. Here the court would decide whether the new policy was so unfair as to amount to a breach of power. **Hamble Fisheries** were cases of this kind.

However the problem with this 'solution' is that, although it makes certain the recognition of the doctrine of substantive legitimate expectations, we do not know the standard of review to be applied. It is mentioned that in type 1, cases are judged by the Wednesbury standard which indicates by implication that the others are to be judged by some other rule. Further, how is one to categorise whether a situation is a type 1 or 3.

The question of decisions within the 'macro-political' field arose again in *Bibi.* The local authority had promised to house a family in legally secure accommodation within 18 months. Subsequently the local authority withdrew the promise. The Court of Appeal proposed a three-stage test for courts to adopt when deciding how

to approach cases involving legitimate expectation:
1) What has the decision-maker committed itself to?;
2) Has the decision maker acted unlawfully or do they propose to do so?;
3) What should the court do?

Recap: Indeed in **Begbi** was made clear that the line is not a clearly marked one, and while certain factors (such as detrimental reliance) point towards it being a type 3, one cannot say for certain. Moreover, what is the standard used in a type 3 case? This is point is still unclear, the language used by the court was that of an abuse of power, although Craig points out that this itself is not a standard of review, but the conclusion the court reaches when applying a certain standard – he suggested that the standards which could be employed are modified Wednesbury and proportionality.

As regards modified Wednesbury, Craig suggests that a test akin to that used when fundamental rights are at stake, demanding more from the public authority before reasonableness will be found. He also states that such a test would require the court to determine why a decision was not reasonable and that the factors to take into account would be akin to proportionality. However, the label we attach to the test is not really of great importance – far more vital is the substance of the test. As with the majority of public law, it becomes an issue of balancing the unfairness of a change in policy which frustrates a legitimate expectation, against whatever overriding public needs there may be in not doing so.

Your arguments for doctrine

Argument 1: Yet despite the criticisms of the standard of judicial review that should be applied under **Coughlan**, the decision to clearly state that legitimate expectations has a place in English law is one which, in my opinion, should be welcomed. Indeed, when dealing with public authorities, individuals are not likely to be merely planning an isolated exercise of any rights they may be afforded under current policy, more likely they will be attempting to conclude ongoing business. On this basis it is vital to the individual concerned that they are able to plan for the future. In order to do this, there must be a certain minimum level of certainty; this is essentially the basis of **Raz's** theories of the Rule of Law. Where a public authority changes policy with immediate effect, it may often prevent an individual from being able to conclude what they have started, and even that which they may have been promised they could finish.

Argument 2: It can be viewed as a matter of fairness that we expect some level of certainty with which we can plan our affairs.

Your arguments against doctrine

Argument 1: The argument against the doctrine is generally that it places a fetter on the discretion of the authority, and if they have been given a statutory duty to use discretion, this may be ultra vires. Such an argument is not particularly convincing, however. Firstly, as we have noted, the importance of certainty is a compelling point. Furthermore, the principle is not a general fetter on the ability of public authorities to change policy, but a fetter on their ability to frustrate legitimate expectations. Where changes in policy are announced with sufficient notice, it is highly unlikely that there would be any legitimate expectations to protect.

Argument 2: Moreover, it is not an absolute principle: there will always be some balancing against the need for the administration to change policy where the circumstances demand it.

Argument 3: Finally, the doctrine has been applicable in most EC member states for a considerable time, and it has not been suggested that it has placed an unreasonable fetter on policy-making when it has been applied.

Sumary

So, then, the doctrine does now seem to stand in English law and will be likely to be invoked in four situations:
1. A general policy is relied on. The policy is changed.
2. An individual representation has been relied on. General policy has changed to deny this.
3. A general policy is relied on, but the public authority departs from this in individual cases.
4. An individual representation is made but the authority changes its mind.

It may be that the doctrine need not be applied rigidly and that the balance could, indeed, be struck differently in these varying situations to reflect the needs of each case. For example in 4, the doctrine is unlikely to be considered controversial: where an individual has been promised something by a governmental body, the idea is that they gain a right to have such carried out, therefore the arguments on fettering general policy would be inapplicable and the promised position ought to apply. The same could be said for 3: the public authority as a matter of fairness should only be allowed to depart from general policy in a particular case, and in unusual circumstances. In 2, the argument on fettering has some force, but it is unlikely to be severely against the public interest to allow the individual to have their promised expectations to be protected, unless the authority has made many such representations. Only in 1 does the balance seem to tip slightly the other way, such that public authority should normally be permitted to change policy unfettered. Even here though, situations like Hamble Fisheries might suggest that the courts have a useful role in preventing unfair policy changes without notice, and in monitoring the existence and satisfactoriness of transitional provisions.

In relation to the question of what the court should do, the Court of Appeal adopted the reasoning in **Begbie**, namely that the more a decision involves social/political value judgments, the less intrusive should be the court's approach. The Court of Appeal also suggested that detrimental reliance would not be essential in establishing legitimate expectation, as this would place the weakest in society at particular disadvantage.

There is considerable academic debate as to whether this should be the standard of review to apply in legitimate expectation cases. In **Niazi/Bhatt Murphy** Laws L.J. reiterated the point he made in **Nadarajah** that legitimate expectation, as part of the principle of good administration, is a constitutional necessity of such importance that it ranks alongside those rights found in the ECHR and, as such, any departure from a legitimate expectation must be justified by reference to proportionality.

Proportionality has been used as the standard of review in a number of subsequent cases including **R. (on the application of**

Fingle Glen Junction Business and Community Action Group) v Highways Agency.

In contrast in **Wheeler** the court, despite having been referred to **Nadarajah,** appeared to suggest that, if the comparison between treaties was justiciable, the only possible basis on which to approach the matter would be on a Wednesbury standard of review. This follows the reasoning in **R. (on the application of Association of British Civilian Internees (Far East Region)) v Secretary of State for Defence** that Wednesbury is the correct test to apply where Community Law and rights under the ECHR are not involved.

It can therefore be seen that without any further judicial guidance on the issue proportionality is now the appropriate standard of review in substantive legitimate expectation cases where Convention rights are raised. Although proportionality can conceivably deal with procedural expectation cases as well, it is harder to fit into the usual analysis and therefore more suited to a Wednesbury unreasonableness standard. Clarification will have to be awaited as the combined effects of **Nadarajah, Wheeler and Bhatt Murphy** are tested through the courts.

Conclusion

So then it would seem that the recognition of substantive legitimate expectations is to be welcomed, but that the standard of review in such cases does indeed remain problematic. However, as noted above, when seeking this standard of review it is not in fact the label that is important, but that the courts perform a principled balancing exercise – using fairness in administration as their guide – between the need to protect legitimate expectations of individuals and, if any, the needs of the public at large.

Printed in Great Britain
by Amazon

81549701R00088